RAISING
JENNIFER
LAWRENCE
AS MOLLY BROWN

A TRUE STORY

BONNIE BROWN

SHADOW MOUNTAIN MEDIA, LLC
Grand Lake, Colorado

Raising Jennifer Lawrence as Molly Brown:
A True Story
Bonnie Brown

Copyright © 2020 by Bonnie Brown

ISBN: 978-1-7330025-7-8 paperback
ISBN: 978-1-7330025-1-6 hardcover
ISBN: 978-1-7330025-2-3 eBook
Library of Congress Control Number: 2019904954

First Edition
Printed in the United States of America

SHADOW MOUNTAIN MEDIA. LLC
Grand Lake, Colorado
shadowmtnmedia.com
JLawsmom.com

DEDICATION

For My Mother
MARY AGNES PETERSON
1926-2017

She went with me to the IRS office holding my hand while witnessing the revelation, Jennifer Shrader Lawrence was her long lost *favorite* grand daughter never forgotten.

Mom was my only supporter until her final days when she whispered to me

"Finish the book Bonnie. Bring our Molly home"

These memories are to the best of my recollection true with correct inciting incidents. Names have been changed for the purpose of telling an honest account of the way I remember events.

"All truth passes through three stages. First, it is ridiculed. Second, it is violently opposed. Third, it is accepted as being self-evident."

–ARTHUR SCHOPENHAUER, German philosopher (1788-1860)

ACKNOWLEDGMENTS

T HIS BOOK HAS BEEN YEARS IN THE MAKING and there have been many instrumental people who have helped me realize its publication.

I would like to express my sincere gratitude to my publishing coach, Mike Daniels, for his guidance, influence, advice and knowledge of the publishing business. Thank you for your direction and vision on how best to publish this incredible journey of truth.

Many thanks to Robert Schram of Bookends Design for his tireless effort creating the interior layout.

To Charol Messenger, my editor, for pulling the heap together and making it readable in spite of my many changes and additions.

To Veronica Yager of YellowStudios, for bringing me into the world of modern technology while creating the eBook version and book cover.

I'm so grateful to Pennie Collinson of Coeur d'Alene Photography for her express camera work and continual support. She helped to give new life to many of the photos found within the book.

I so appreciate Steve Litt who has supported me emotionally before, during and after Molly/Jennifer vanished.

To Jack Castle, for noticing me in your class and putting the notion in my head that I should write a book.

I truly value my friendship with Anna Goodwin and the support and knowledge that I gleaned from her as a psychotherapist helped me to understand the underpinnings of mental illness.

To my Grand Lake friends, Dave Freeman at the Sagebrush and Lin Long of the Pearl Dragon both of whom Molly worked for as a teenager growing up.

To Cathy Walton-Smith for encouraging my family to move me to Idaho and longtime friend, Craig Capps for his unselfish support when I needed it the most.

I am forever grateful to my prayer warriors, Deb Ganz and Cecilia Hudson in Memphis for always holding me up. "God's Got This!"

Lastly, to my brother, Philip Peterson, with my sincere appreciation for believing in me while allowing me to live with him through these last few months during book production.

To quote Pastor Rogers' refrain at Bellevue Baptist, *I thank you all for helping me "eat my elephant one bite at a time."*

CONTENTS

Letter to My Beloved Daughter
Dear Molly, Dear Jen

PART II
Starting My Career As a Chef
(Love and Marriage)

PART III
Molly's Childhood

PART IV
Molly Style

Letter to My Beloved Daughter

Dear Molly, Dear Jen

G IVING WITHOUT EXPECTATION is my goal in writing this book. I hope and release these words into the universe, asking for prayerful compassion, understanding and empathy as to why the life-altering decisions were made that determined our divine destinies.

I feel it is my responsibility and my honor as your mother to help your audience understand who *Jennifer Shrader Lawrence* really is: where you were born, who are your real parents, and who is your long-lost brother Cody.

In these pages, I share our family history, capturing the stories of your youth to age fifteen and losing your father far too soon.

Let me reminisce and reflect, from my perspective, how you ended up in Kentucky after you didn't get off the plane at Denver International Airport (DIA) in June 2006. Allow me to soften the blow as I explain what truly happened to you, my daughter, born Molly Mackenzie Brown in the early morning hours of April 9, 1991 in Portland, Oregon.

As you were so young, I include here photographs of your young life, captured by your daddy JJ and me in Vancouver, Washington; Scottsdale, Arizona; Cordova, Tennessee; and of course, our beloved Grand Lake, Colorado.

It is my wish to shed some truths while explaining the circumstances in which you carefully, systematically protected your past as you bravely forged ahead, believing the path you had chosen was the correct one.

And perhaps it was! Because look at you now! You are amazing.

Nevertheless, I still miss you. And I am so sorry for anything I didn't do to be there for you. I am sorry you had to make that decision alone. I know you were scared. Too many grown-up decisions for a girl of your young age. You had to be brave while learning the life skills you needed to survive, separated from your mother.

Because of your courage, determination and, yes, DNA you created a *make-believe* world to protect you from those who governed over you, who gave little heed as to how they were impacting you.

I more than applaud you. You are my hero!

Decisions were made that did not help you in your all-important teen years when one usually makes lasting friendships in high school. However, in spite of missing out on double-dates, dances, prom, homecoming and a graduation day, you have fared very well and these experiences pale in comparison to winning an Oscar, a much-coveted different type of award.

I feel you may think God abandoned you when your father passed. That is one of my reasons for writing this book, in case I am taken abruptly as well. We never know his plan for us. I had no idea he would put people in my path to help me find a way to reach out to you in this way. But he knew, and I give him all the credit, glory, and honor. He wouldn't have shown me how to write these precious memories for you unless he had a plan in mind, and I get the honor of sharing it with you, your fans and our friends. What a great blessing this has bestowed on me and I pray you feel the same way.

You must have asked yourself, how could God let one of the most important people in your life pass at age fifty-nine? One minute, your father didn't pick you up at school, the next he was taken away in an ambulance, us never getting to hear his voice again.

I, too, lost your father to the brain cancer, right before we were to *remarry* the summer of 2005. Then one year later, you went missing. It was just too much for me, so I drank and drank.

I have been alcohol free for over ten years now and today I help other women face their own demons. I mentor and give talks to all who will listen, on a different stage than you. I think you'll be proud.

Together, we remember JJ's voice as he once sang out. He made us laugh at his funny gruff voice, the same one you imitated on *David Letterman:* "Have a Holly Jolly Christmas." I saw that on YouTube. I knew instantly who you were imitating. We both miss him. Now let's honor him.

I noticed you pay homage to your father by adding an extra J in your autograph. Jennifer Lawrence doesn't have two "J's". I get it. And on your Internet Movie Database (IMBD) page Jennifer Shrader Lawrence the III (third?). And the two J's you added to your chin in a posted photograph. A mother's love for her daughter notices these things. I love you that much, paying attention to these clues to your identity, after searching for you for so long.

But first I had to get sober. Once I surrendered, I became sober, with Grandma's nurturing ways when I moved in with her while recovering.

It's been over ten years since I left Colorado. I know what it feels like living with your mother, especially a senior one. Do you remember spending time at her house in Idaho, riding around in the golf cart, golfing with Grandma and your uncle?

Motherhood is a job
Given only to the strong
The ones who know how to care
And teach right from wrong.

It's for the patient women
Who are kind and wise
Who can look upon their children
With gentle, loving eyes.

It's for the ones who know
How to mend a broken heart
Who look at children's scribbles

And see the finest a t

It's not a job that's easy
But its rewards are great
When you look upon that child's smile
That you helped to create.

Happy Mother's Day to a wonderful mother!

Happy Mother's Day
- J

Then my best day in a very long time, January 30, 2018. We were privately chatting on Facebook messenger, when you wrote, "I love you, too."

That's when I knew it was time to move forward with publishing this book, during your year off from acting. Something you were thinking about perhaps when you said I had inspired you to take action? I hope you meant you're ready to reunite as I take this chance of sharing our stories.

Your Grand Lake friends have never forgotten you. We are all still waiting for you to come home. We remain with a light in the window.

I love you, Molly Girl. Oh, I mean . . . Jennifer!
See you soon.
Mom.

CHAPTER ONE

Losing My Daughter

I HAD JUST GOTTEN OFF THE PHONE with Molly, June 2006. She was fifteen and in Tennessee visiting her daddy JJ.

One year ago, she had found out he had brain cancer. No one knew at the time it was terminal. If we had, perhaps our lives would have been much different.

I now chalk it up to destiny. If these horrific series of events hadn't happened the way they did, maybe Jennifer Lawrence never would have become the famous actress she is.

"Molly," I said over the phone, "you don't seem very excited about coming home."

"It's just so hard, and I'm scared."

"Molly, honey, your daddy will live on forever in our hearts and minds. Sweetheart, everything will be fine. Now, be very careful when you get on the plane with your daddy's ashes. Just focus on the box you're carrying. It's all we have left of him, aside from our memories. It's not a large box, is it?"

"No," she said quietly.

"Think about all the trips on the planes we took with your daddy JJ. And he's with you again on this one. Bring him back to me, Molly. Bring your daddy home." My heart filled with the immense loss of him, as we were just about to remarry. My voice broke as I added, "I miss you so much, Molly. I just can't stand any longer you're being away. You've been gone too long. Let's just think of your time in Tennessee as an extension of your summer vacation, and now it's time to return home to Colorado and get back on track. All of your friends in Grand Lake are waiting for you, Molly. I'm waiting for you. We can have another slumber party at the Lodge if you want."

"Okay." Silence. "I . . . I don't want to think about that right now. . . Don't you have to start driving from the cabin?"

"Yes, but I just wanted to make sure everything is in place. And I wanted to hear your voice. Driving through the mountains to DIA, I won't have many bars on the cell, so I just wanted to check in with you and comfort you. You already have your return flight ticket, and I've signed you up for an unaccompanied minor escort."

"Yeah, I know, Mom. I don't need a babysitter. I *am* fifteen now."

"Honey, I realize that. It's just that you're my precious cargo and I need you to arrive here safely with no worries."

"No worries, Mom. I have to hang up now. Love you."

"Love you more."

Those were the last words I spoke to my daughter that day nearly thirteen years ago.

As I drove through Berthoud Pass in the Land Rover, I listened to one of Molly's favorite CDs, artists from EMI/Virgin Records. Now that's what I call music!

Though even with reveling in the music, I couldn't get down the mountain pass quickly enough. My precious Molly Girl was returning to her home of the last five years in Grand Lake! I couldn't wait to have her activity in the house again.

I had just cleaned her room and reorganized her clothes into a new dresser I bought for her as a surprise, plus a new desk and office chair. It would be more efficient now that she was entering tenth grade, something more grown up than the one riddled with her stickers from childhood. She was in high school now for the 2005-06 school year at Middle Park High School in Granby.

As I drove down the 175-mile trip one-way to DIA, I reminisced about the day in July 1990, when I had come here the week before JJ and I were to marry, to make the arrangements for our wedding at Grand Lake.

Now our daughter was bringing him home in a box. Tears streamed down my face.

I looked at my watch. Only four more hours and my precious girl would be by my side again.

I had another surprise for her, too, a quick shopping trip to Cherry Creek Plaza in Denver so she could pick up a few new summer clothes. She would like that, and we could have a bite to eat afterwards.

The minutes ticked away as I made my way down I-70, then onto the new turnpike that drops you right at the door at Denver International Airport.

Such a desolate drive on the new turnpike, so new it was barren, nothing but prairie. I thought of the cute little mountain prairie dogs and all the holes they make. Molly, too, always thought they were cute.

Finally, I found a parking place on one of the lower levels, then hurried into the airport. I made sure I had my driver's license so I could claim Molly at the check-out counter, since she was a minor. One year I had left my ID in the car and had to go all the way back—through the tunnel, onto the shuttle, then back to the arrival gate. I wouldn't do that again.

I checked the flight schedules. *Good, good,* I said to myself, and synchronized my watch. It was too late to call Molly one more time, to make sure she had gotten on the flight. I excitedly pushed my way through the crowed terminal to the underground train shuttle. How much the airport had changed since my first flights back and forth from Memphis to Denver!

Then with a moment of sharp realization, I remembered that the last time I was here at the airport JJ was still *alive*.

In fact, I had done this same adventure *last* June when I put Molly on the plane to go be with him in Cordova, Tennessee, a district of Memphis. At the time, he and I were divorced and Molly wanted to be with her daddy.

Then he was diagnosed with the brain tumor, the size of a grapefruit.

Right after they removed it in June 2005, what they could, he had called me from his hospital bed. "BB, why aren't we married anymore?" And we made plans to remarry next month, in July.

Grateful that her dad had survived the surgery and was back to himself again, Molly was planning our wedding party, as I had a business to run at Grand Lake, my boutique gift shop The Flannel Antler. I would join them the following month on my and JJ's fifteenth anniversary.

I didn't know then he would be gone in six weeks and there would no second marriage to the man to whom I had devoted my life.

I made it to the arrival gate. At least that's what I thought.

I was still surprised at how many people were departing and arriving to Denver from Memphis. Why would anyone choose to go to Memphis? When I was there, I couldn't wait to leave. I had always dreamed of returning to my beautiful newlywed cabin in Vancouver, Washington; Molly had been born in the hospital nearby in Portland, Oregon. I had kept in touch with the couple who bought the cabin, which JJ had built for me as a wedding present. They had promised me that if they ever decided to sell, they would offer it back to me and I would get first right of refusal. This had kept me going, because one day I was going to buy back that cabin and live in it again. Now, I had been away since 1994, twelve years, and the reasons I had wanted it were fading.

It seemed like an eternity as I sat there waiting for Molly's plane from Memphis. When it landed and was taxiing to the gate, I went to the picture window and pressed my face against it, trying to see if her window seat was facing me. I walked the entire length of the window.

Hmm, I thought, *she must be on the other side of the plane. Or maybe they had room in First Class since she's an unaccompanied minor.* She would love that. She'd order one of everything.

The time finally arrived. One by one, the passengers filed off the plane. Minors were usually brought off first, with a hostess assigned to them. I had sent an extra hundred for that.

More people piled off, then a few more stragglers. Then no one else was getting off the plane. And no Molly.

Confused, I checked the flight reader board. Yes, I was at the right gate. I was waiting, fresh daisies in hand. I looked around. I was where I was supposed to be. Where was Molly?

Then the pilot and hostess came down the ramp. And the woman at the ticket counter locked up and she, too, started to walk away. I ran over and grabbed her by the arm. "Where's Molly"?

Startled, she stepped back. "What?"

"Where's Molly? My daughter was on the flight and she hasn't gotten off yet." I ran up the ramp, past the pilot. "Molly! Molly!"

He dropped his bag and caught up with me. "Miss, there's no one left on the plane. I'm the last one."

"Oh, no, you're not! My Molly is on the plane! I paid for an unaccompanied minor. Where's my daughter?"

He took me back to the ticket counter. "This woman says her daughter was on the flight. Let's look at the manifest."

"I've already closed out the flight," the clerk said. "There's no one left."

"Let's reopen it," he said, "and see if we can find her daughter."

I frantically tried to call Cathy, a friend of JJ's from church, with whom Molly had been staying since his death. Two hours ago Cathy had told me she put Molly on the plane.

But I had no cell reception.

I totally panicked now. Had Molly slipped by me? Had I missed her? Was she looking for me?

"OH, MY GOD, WHERE'S MOLLY?" I wailed, full on crying.

"No, sir," the clerk said to the pilot, "there weren't any unaccompanied minors on this flight."

"YES, THERE WAS!" I shouted. "MOLLY!"

I rambled on about how I had sent the money two weeks ago and I knew for a fact they had received it, and how it was a big deal for me to be here on time *before* her flight arrived.

"What's her name?" the pilot asked. "Date of birth? Who put her on the plane?"

"Cathy put her on the plane. It was a return ticket from a flight a year ago to Memphis. This was the return portion of the ticket."

I nearly collapsed. "And now her daddy's dead," I said, my voice shaking, "and the lady she's been staying with put her on the plane."

The clerk looked at the pilot. "Maybe we can find her from the initial plane departure and track her that way?"

Soon a couple of security guards were also at the counter, and they all huddled together as I stood in horror, crying my heart out.

Then the clerk did find Molly in the computer. "Yes, Molly Mackenzie Brown, age fourteen."

"Now fifteen," I said.

The pilot looked at the screen, too. The security guards looked at the screen, too. Then they all turned to me. "Ma'am," the clerk said, "the second half of the ticket was never redeemed."

I stood there for an eternity. I had just talked to Cathy. I collapsed in a seat. "I don't understand."

The pilot asked the security guards to take me to their station office where we could get an outside line to call Cathy and find out where Molly was.

Back through the underground tunnel was the longest ride. Mascara streamed down my face. The daisies for Molly were limp. "Where's Molly?" I sobbed.

At the security station, they called Cathy's number, long distance. We got a recording. They hung up, then tried again. Same thing.

I slouched in a chair, listening to the recording repeating, "I am sorry. This number is no longer in service, and there is no new number."

No longer in service? I stared at the cement wall.

"Ma'am, ma'am, do you have a different number we can try?"

"No. That's the only number I have for Molly." I stood up and walked out of the office like a zombie.

I finally found my car. I tried Cathy's phone number one more time. Same thing. Disconnected.

I drove out of the parking garage, not knowing where I was going or what I was going to do.

Then I had an thought. When I had lived in Memphis, my best friend Sissy had gone with me a couple of times to pick up Molly at Cathy's house where she was hanging out with Cathy's fourteen-year-old daughter. It had been obvious to both Sissy and me, even then, that Cathy had wanted to be JJ's girlfriend.

I pulled off the road just outside the airport parking garage, alongside the vast prairie land. No one else was around, just the prairie dogs. I immediately called Sissy and, luckily, she answered!

"Sissy!" I said in a panic, sweating. "Molly didn't get on the plane! And Cathy's not answering her phone! It's been disconnected! Molly wasn't on the plane like Cathy said! Please, Sissy, do you remember how to get over there?"

"Yes, I think so."

"Please, I beg you. Go to Cathy's house and find out what happened, and tell her the phone's not working."

"Okay, no problem. I'll call you right back."

I waited and waited, watching cars go by, and the prairie dogs, and the sun set. Finally, my cell phone rang.

"Bonnie, I hate to tell you this. They're not there."

I gasped. "The cars weren't there?"

"No." Long pause. "No one's there. The house is vacant."

"What? I just talked to Molly four hours ago. Maybe you have the wrong house?"

"No, Bonnie. I asked a neighbor. They haven't seen anyone for a while. They moved out."

"Oh, my God. Sissy, Molly's been kidnapped!"

"You need to call the police."

It was a very somber drive back up the mountain to Grand Lake, without my little girl, another 175 long miles all the way back.

At home by dark, I sluggishly walked inside the front door to Boo-Boo jumping up on me, Molly's six-pound white Miniature Poodle, asking me, *Where's Molly?*

I picked her up and hugged her tightly. "Molly's not here, Boo-Boo. They took her."

I walked through the house in the dark, poured myself a big glass of wine, went into Molly's bedroom and flicked on the lights, Boo-Boo at my feet. The "Welcome Home" balloons and banner from her friends seemed to sag, too.

"No, Boo, Molly's not here." I chucked down the wine. "And I don't know where she is."

Crying, I slumped to the floor against Molly's bed, where Boo-Boo comforted me.

When Molly was still a baby in 1991, JJ had bought the puppy for her at a pet shop in Memphis. But it was really a bribe to me to move from our newlywed log house in Vancouver, Washington to awful Memphis, Tennessee, where he had just gotten a new job after being fired for sexual harassment from Portland's Red Lions headquarters as their lead architect. A man of his profession couldn't find another job making $250,000 a year where we were, so he'd hired headhunters and the only position that interviewed him was Davidson Hotel Corporation in Memphis.

As we were emotionally separated at the time, though still living in same house with our baby, JJ simply said to me this would give us a fresh start—and I believed him, enough to do what was best for my baby girl and my little boy.

The truth was, we were moving to the Bible Belt and JJ needed a wife and children to fit the profile they required, as they had made it clear they would not hire someone single or divorced. JJ also had convinced me that if I did divorce him, I couldn't afford the mortgage for the Vancouver cabin mansion on my own. The truth was he had two boat payments of $60,000 and a car payment of $40,000 and he couldn't afford his luxurious lifestyle and also pay me alimony and child support.

I hugged Boo-Boo against me, both of us grieving for Molly.

"She's lost, Boo, and I don't know how to find her."

My fluffy little friend whimpered and looked up at me with her big sad eyes.

That night was the night my light left me.

CHAPTER TWO

Discovering My Passion
for Cooking

W HAT IF YOU'RE TAUGHT NOT TO QUESTION your father's authority, ever, or suffer the consequences of a severe beating? Imagine growing up with the belief that you never question a man, that what he says is gospel, and that you have to accept it as such.

This was beat into me, literally, more than once.

I remember one time in particular when I was thirteen, a freshman in the ninth grade, nearly the same age as Molly when, at fifteen, she surrendered to her uncle's decision to hide her away from me.

My dad's routine was very predictable: Monday, Wednesday, and Friday nights were his drinking nights. Tuesdays and Thursdays were his recuperation days.

We four siblings watched him knock down a six-pack of Coors every night. During the week, he'd get home around four p.m. and the beers were gone by six.

When dinner was nearly ready, Mom timed it to around the finish of his fifth can of beer. Then we'd begin our nightly ritual: all siblings washing our hands, then our setting-the-table dance as we watched Dad until he'd downed the sixth beer. We couldn't start eating until all six beers were gone.

All too often, he'd nurse the last one because he knew the buzz he was feeling would subside after he popped one morsel of food into his mouth. That is one thing I learned from my dad: Drink until you can drink no more, because your party will end if your lips touch a morsel of food.

Mom did her best to time the completion of cooking with his last gulp. Sometimes it didn't work out this way, and that's when I was sent in. My job was to charm my daddy, by saying whatever story I made up to convince him to join us at the table. I couldn't let my siblings down. They'd blame me if it took too long to persuade him.

As our supper grew colder and colder, waiting for us at the dinner table, waiting for Dad to come off his bar stool and join us, Mom would make us sit there, looking at our food, clean hands in our laps, staring at Dad, whose back was turned away from us.

My older brother Vern would poke me. "Make him sit."

"Please, Daddy," I'd beg.

Night after night, I was burdened, trying to figure out a trick or what to say to get Daddy to the table. Did that experience teach me how to be creative and how to say whatever is necessary to get a man to do what I want? I have often wondered this.

"Please, Daddy, sit down at the table with us. It's okay if you're not hungry—but we are. Mom won't let us start 'til you sit down with us," I'd coax. I'd say anything to make him budge.

He'd grumble and sometimes slap at me. "Go away. Let me finish my beer."

"Daddy, please. My stomach hurts. I'm tired and I want to go to bed. Please sit down. Come on."

I'd grab him one last time until I convinced him and lovingly led him to sit at the head of the table so we could all begin our dinner.

Other times, I'd wrap my arms around his neck, kiss him on his cheek and squeeze him, confessing how much I loved him. "I love you, Daddy. Come sit with us," I'd beg. "I have something very important to tell you at dinner tonight."

I'd whisper in his ear, smelling the stank refuse of the beer on his breath. He always smelled like alcohol. It was his signature scent, emanating from him; combined with Old Spice aftershave and stale cigarette smoke. The billowing smoke would choke me. I'd try to hold my breath around the cigarettes, but it was difficult because both Mom and Dad had a cigarette lit at all times.

So, I could never convince myself to drink beer or even to smell one for that matter. My younger brother Phil did adopt Old Spice in manhood. That's not all he copied. After Dad's death, he morphed into our father, carrying on tirades in the same manner, as if Dad's spirit of meanness had entered my brother's soul.

When we finally sat at the dinner table, after much song and dance on my part, Dad would take his last swig, belch and crumple up the can in his mighty fist. "Ah, that was good."

Often it was late into the evening before we were allowed to eat our dinner.

We were always hungry.

My older brother Vern, older sister Lorraine, and the youngest my brother Phil were never expected to sweet-talk Daddy into joining us at the table. It was always my job, because they already had done their parts: Lorraine started the dinner for Mom every night, so when she got home from her job as a government civil servant, it didn't take much time to open a can of vegetables or butter the white Wonder bread. Vern's job was setting the table. Phil was too young to have any chores. He was the baby and Mom's favorite; she'd had him when she was thirty-six and I was seven. We just had to make sure he didn't hurt himself or get into any mischief.

In the morning, our bowls of cold cereal lasted long enough for a quick sugar rush, which burned off within an hour. Lunch was either a brown-bagged peanut-butter-and-jelly sandwich, or a hot school lunch when money allowed. After-school snacks were nonexistent, unless we went into the groves and picked an avocado or an orange off a tree in season, outrunning the farmer who owned the trees. Those were the days when we lived in the city of Yorba Linda in sunny California, where I grew up.

Dinners weren't extraordinary, pretty much the same Monday through Friday. Mondays, *slumgullion*, a Slovenian staple my grandma had taught my mom to make; made with elbow macaroni, canned tomato and some hamburger with a little salt n' pepper. Wednesdays, pork n' beans, fried sliced potatoes, and hamburger gravy. Fridays, fish, which meant canned tuna with noodles (it wasn't called pasta then), mixed with a can of Campbell's Cream of Mushroom soup. Tuesdays and Thursdays were leftovers from the night before, with a canned vegetable, like spinach (Dad's favorite), vinegar, salt n' pepper; sometimes, canned tomato with a teaspoon of sugar. That was the only way I'd eat tomatoes. I had to struggle through that awful slumgullion twice a week, which was enough tomato for me; or a can of corn or peas on tuna-noodle night. We didn't have dessert, except popcorn on rare occasion, a cheap dessert for a family of six.

Weekends, we never knew what we were going to eat. There wasn't a school lunch we could count on. We usually made baloney sandwiches.

Saturdays, we did make some mighty fine meals. Foods I liked. Dad would flip through his big green book of recipes.

"What are we going to make today?" I'd asked with anticipation.

Most times, he'd make cream puffs. They were incredible! Even if it meant extra dish duty, worth it! As we seldom had dessert, it was extraordinary! But, mostly, Dad made green chili for burritos.

Both Saturday and Sunday mornings, Dad made Mom cook us a big farm breakfast—a hearty, fatty meal to cure his weekend hangovers. It was always a hot breakfast with eggs, potatoes, bacon or sausage, and homemade Bisquick biscuits with jelly; topped off with fresh-squeezed orange juice, from oranges that either Vern or Lorraine nabbed off the farmer's trees. Sometimes on Sundays after church, Mom made thin pancakes, a Slovenian delicacy.

Then as soon as breakfast was done, chores. Saturdays were Mom's wash day. She and I would strip all the beds in the four-bedroom, two-bath country house in Yorba Linda, gather up all the dirty clothes and take them to the garage where Mom did the washing in the Sears Kenmore. Then we hung out everything on the five clotheslines.

Dad never allowed Mom to buy a clothes dryer. I never understood why, since Mom was the bread winner of the family. In fact, she hung out the clothes all the way up to age sixty-one (younger than I am now), until after Dad died in 1988.

Though I must admit, there's nothing like a sheet that is blown-dry by the sunny southern California air wafting with the aroma of fresh orange blossoms.

Painstakingly, Mom and I would carry the plastic laundry basket with our clothespins, and pin each bedsheet to the clotheslines along the side of the house.

Under those clotheslines, I had many a conversation with my mom as we waited for the laundry to dry, sharing secrets even though other chores still had to be done. As we hung one piece of clothing after the next, Mom tried to convince me that all men were like my dad, drinking one night, recuperating the next.

One time, I even let her in on a big secret I had been keeping. I was thoroughly disgusted with having to dry dish after dish. "I might have to do the dishes now," I proclaimed boldly, "dry them and put them away. But when I grow up, I will never have to wash another dish."

"Oh, why is that?" she asked with a smile.

"I will have servants to do that for me."

I was dead serious. A girl's gotta dream.

I think I got my own future and my daughter's mixed up. LOL. I'll bet Molly's never washed a dish since she left home in 2006. Though I know she loved my cooking.

We four children all had chores every day. We had to clean both bathrooms, dust mop all the bedroom floors to get the *mauchka,* the bohemian name for dust bunnies, out from under the beds and off the linoleum floors. We also had to dust the furniture with Lemon Pledge, vacuum the living room, then mop the kitchen floor. As the eldest, Vern's job was to mow the front and back yards.

Mom got great pleasure from tending her many flowers that lined the perimeter of our country house, in-between doing loads of laundry. She was a master gardener, filling our backyard with orange and purple Birds of Paradise, yellow and purple Pansies, Monkey faces, and under my bedroom window the small white fragrant blossoms of Night Blooming Jasmine. She lined the perimeter stucco walls with tall white lilies, red and pink geraniums, pink rhododendron bushes, pink bougainvillea, and blue powder-puff hydrangeas. In the front yard, we had a date palm tree and a huge weeping willow. Plus, to my delight, the farmer's orange grove surrounded the right side of our house. The avocado orchard was behind us.

Dad and Me

Dad and I were born two days apart in September. Mom always said I was his birthday gift. We certainly shared a love for good and unique food. No one else in the family cared, but Dad and I could cook all day on Saturdays, if Mom let us. That's when I developed my love for cooking. It gave me great pleasure.

Although Dad tended his own tomato plants, he was fat, bloated, and overweight the entire time I knew him, probably the beer.

I wasn't fat. I was pretty though an average 5'4', not too short but I certainly didn't get the Peterson long legs Molly/Jennifer did.

In California, Dad delivered fresh produce door-to-door up and down the streets of Orange County, despite having lost a hand at age eighteen in a gun accident when living at "Boys Town" in Iowa.

He converted a pickup into a moving produce-stand. Mondays through Fridays, he drove to the L.A. Farmers Market to buy goods at one a.m. Then he began his route.

However, that wasn't enough to support his family, so he also got a job at Stouffers, when they were the new kind of TV dinner food service. He lost that job when he got his second D.U.I., driving from the bar in Brea, called "Bunny's."

For a while in the 1970s, he was the custodian at my high school Valencia. Then until he died in 1988, he worked at a liquor store in Santa Ana, close to where Mom was working, at that time teletyping classified documents for the Department of Defense.

During my high-school years, Dad missed more days from work than he worked. We didn't know that he would die just a few years later.

Mom and Dad were both in their fifties when I was in high school. They were old and old-fashioned.

I can't even imagine, now, how some men are thinking about starting their families at age fifty. Molly was born when JJ was forty-six, and he fought me tooth-and-nail about giving birth to her.

Most Friday nights, Dad fell asleep drunk at the kitchen counter *after* we were in bed and weren't bringing him anymore beer or ashtrays.

He'd wake up about five a.m. and shout my name in his drunken babble, "Bonnie! Bonnie! Where are you! You ungrateful bitch!"

I was his favorite subservient.

I would be sound asleep, barely enough sleep after waiting on him 'til late at night.

"Bonnie! Bonnie!"

If I didn't answer, he had his ritual. First, he'd come into my bedroom and shout my name, "Bonnie! It's time to rise and shine!" He'd annoyingly flip the lights on and off.

If that didn't wake me, it was Plan B. He'd go into the kitchen, fill the biggest glass he could find with ice-cold water. Bumping back down the hallway, still drunk, he'd walk into my room, shouting, "Last call! Time for all little girls to wake up!"

He'd stand over me, while I was still sound asleep and pour the ice-cold water all over my face and head.

Now I know how I got my insomnia.

I'd wake up in a panic, gasping. This also alerted the whole house. Better get up.

Then Mom would yell at me. "Clean up this mess!" As though I were the one. "Clean up that wet bed and sheets!"

"But, Mom, it's Saturday and I'm still tired."

"Now!"

At those times, I thought she hated me or resented me. It made me feel I wasn't even her daughter. I guess she had to take it out on someone other than Dad.

CHAPTER THREE

Almost In a Commercial

W HEN I WAS NINE, when Mom was working for the Department of Defense in Santa Ana, California, one
day she received a notice: Hollywood was asking for all em-
ployees to sign up their young children, extra money for putting us on TV. All civil-service workers were to bring their
children to Hollywood to see if we qualified to act in a com-
mercial promoting margarine, the new butter: "Call this
number now for your chance at fame and fortune."

In the early 1960s, people thought about things like com-
merce and getting rich, everyone's fight to achieve the
American Dream. My folks had done pretty well for them-
selves. They had built the beautiful knotty-pine cabin in
Grand Lake, Colorado as a summer cottage. They lived in
Southern California, a stone's throw from the beaches and
the mountains. They were proud of their accomplishments.

My older siblings were too old for the new butter com-
mercial, and my little brother too young at three, so they
sent me. Grandma Popish (Mom's mom) was visiting us
from Colorado. It was the first time she'd seen our house in
Yorba Linda. When people would come to visit from Colorado, Mom took them to Hollywood to see the Grauman's
Chinese Theater, the LaBrea Tarpits, and China Town of
course. (Who knew that my own daughter one day would

have her hand prints cast in stone at the theatre where we had visited?)

Mom made an appointment for me at one of the casting calls. Everyone had always told my mom that I looked like Hailey Mills from *The Moon Spinners*, an English girl with a pug nose just like mine. Relatives always made me feel special when they came to visit. They only paid attention to me, "the cute one," they'd say. Mom thought I was a shoe-in.

But she failed to explain to me *why* we were at this Hollywood movie set and what I was supposed to do—which was *act*.

I had never been to Hollywood. I had no idea there was more to television than John Wayne movies or an occasional *I Love Lucy* show. That must have been before commercials were commonplace or not obvious, because I was clueless.

We waited in a very long line, women and their children standing in the hot sun. Someone occasionally walked up and down the line and pointed to a few of us children. "That one. That one. Yes, she'll work." We put on big smiles as they passed by.

Finally, when I thought I could stand no more, one of the men came by. "Oh, yes. Forgot about you. You, come with me." He grabbed my hand.

Mom and Grandma followed, along the trail of bodies up the stair, into a dark cinematic room.

We all sat there, I in my Sunday dress and bonnet. Squirming, I asked, "What are we doing here? This isn't Disneyland."

I kept thinking we were going to get on a ride. Mom and Grandma kept swiping at me. "Sit up straight. Get off the floor. Sit in your chair."

Mom scolded me. "You're going to get your dress dirty."

"For what?" I asked.

"One of these nice men is going to take you into a room and have a look at you."

"Oh, great," I said, thinking, *They've tricked me. We're at a doctor's office.* But I wasn't sick. *Hmm.* I sighed. I was along for the ride anyway.

Pretty soon, they called me, another girl and two boys. A man pointed at a dinner table. "Sit there."

Oh, that was nice of them. I was hungry.

Plates, napkins, and silverware were at six place settings for us four kids plus a lady at one end and a man at the other.

Soon, the room filled with several adults, some with big cameras. "Role 'em," the director said.

I looked around quizzically, wondering when they were going to bring the food.

Lots of commotion was going on in the back. A man pointed to me, while holding up a cue card that said, PASS THE BUTTER, PLEASE.

A lady behind me poked me in the back. "Come on, say it." She poked me again, this time harder. The cue card was presented to me again.

"Okay, stop!" the director said. "Can't you read, little girl?"

"Sure, I can read!"

"Well, then, read it!" He went back behind the cameraman. "Role 'em!"

A click snapped in the background and the cue card was presented once again. I had already read it. The poking started again. I shoved myself back from the table and pointed my finger at the woman. "You need to stop poking me, lady. I already read the stupid que card. Where's my mom?" What did a girl have to do to get something to eat?

They should have cast me immediately as the latest version of Shirley Temple, but they just wanted me to say the words, *Pass the butter.* It was absurd. Because there wasn't any butter on the table.

"Get her out of here!" the director shouted, and they briskly ushered me out a side door.

Mom and Grandma looked at me as if they'd just lost a million-dollar lottery ticket. "What's the matter with you?" Mom said.

"Me? They're crazy. They wanted me to pass the butter, and the butter wasn't even in front of me. They just kept shoving signs in my face. They were mean! And they didn't even give me any food." I started crying.

After we left, Mom explained that I was supposed to *pretend* there was butter on the table, that it was a game we were playing.

Silly game.

And there went my opportunity to make my parents rich.

That night, after a day of eating Chinese food and looking at mud and fossils at the tar pits, Dad was waiting for us. "Well, how much money are we going to get?" he asked Mom, like he knew I would be the next child star.

"Stupid assholes," she said, shoving me into the living room. "It didn't quite work out."

"What?" He doubled up his fist. "I oughta . . ."

Mom grabbed his hand and lowered it, so Grandma wouldn't see as she entered the kitchen.

"It just didn't work out is all," Mom said, as she immediately began the finishing touches on tonight's dinner, so Dad wouldn't get too drunk in front of her mom.

Not another word was said about what should have been a life-changing day for my family.

If only they had told me it was just a game, I would have charmed them like I always did my daddy—and I would never have had to dry a wet dish again.

CHAPTER FOUR

My Creativity Blossoming

I N HIGH SCHOOL, I was excited that home economics was a requirement. I enjoyed learning how to make goldenrod eggs and biscuits from scratch. I learned of recipes Mom didn't make, because they took too much time, sifting, measuring, and baking. She needed quick and easy meals that could be prepared in less than thirty minutes. So all the meals we ate were mostly three meals, with only three ingredients. Cheap and quick.

I didn't eat a salad with honey-mustard dressing until my senior prom. Oh, my God, it was to die for.

On occasion, mostly on the weekends when there was more time, I'd pester Mom to let me make a box cake with Jiffy icing. It was about the only thing I knew how to make. Just add oil and eggs to the cake mix, put it in the greased pan for a half an hour, and you had a sugary treat for dessert.

"Please, Mom. Please let me make a cake so we can have dessert tonight." I'd wildly clap my hands and jump up and down, hoping for attention. I'd wear her down with my relentless pestering as she was frying hamburger for the evening meal.

"You know the drill, Bonnie. If I let you make a cake, you have to clean up the mess."

I didn't mind. My older sister Lorraine had dish duty every night. Anyway, what was an extra bowl, egg beaters, and a couple of cake pans?

Very rarely did we get dessert, because those dishes had to be done, and who wants to go back into the kitchen and do more dishes at eight p.m.

At the beginning of summer, Mom would drive me to my grandma's house in Colorado. She'd pick me up at the end of summer to spend two weeks working on the cabin in Grand Lake. She'd leave me in Denver to work for my grandparents to earn money for my school clothes.

In 1967 when I was twelve, Grandma Popish taught me how to sew, using her treadle machine. We'd walk to the five-and-dime and she would let me pick out fabric with the money I was earning. I especially loved the blue-and-green paisleys. She picked out a simple sixties sheath-dress to start me on.

We opened the pattern and the directions, but she laid the pattern onto the fabric differently than the directions indicated. "But Grandma, that's not where it says to put that piece." I looked at her quizzically, thinking we were building a puzzle of sorts and it had to match exactly.

"That's right, they just want you to waste fabric. They're in cahoots with the fabric people," she said sternly, grimacing that anyone would waste a single inch of fabric.

Beginning in the tenth grade, I worked after school at the Fabric Boutique, a local fabric store. At age sixteen, I was able to purchase a small red MG convertible with my own money.

The summer of 1968, Grandma showed me how to make a purse with a remnant piece. We went back and purchased a piece of fringe and a little gold chain so it could be a shoulder sling. We made a couple of other dresses, too, and I learned to love sewing. It was my only creative outlet. I blossomed after that.

The summer of 1969, I got a job making $100 a week babysitting three little girls, ages seven, five, and three. I got a boyfriend, too.

I wasn't *allowed* to date until I was in college and eighteen. I was barely allowed to leave my yard, only to go to school or work. Then I had to come straight home.

But once I was in high school, Dad lost control of me—and his drinking got worse and worse. Maybe it was because he started drinking whiskey, which made him crazy. I stayed away from him as much as possible. Because he would chase me with a butcher knife down the middle of the street late at night, hallucinating that I had encouraged the neighborhood boys who were caught peeping into my window at night. I'd run to our neighbor's house, out of breath, barely escaping the ravages of my father. Tanya would let me spend the night.

The summer of 1970, I worked part-time at the Fabric Boutique, earning $1.35 an hour. I'd ride the bus to the shopping center. Once I'd done all my store chores—fabric folded, trim, in order—the owner let me lay out my own pattern onto the large sewing table, where I was the one who cut the fabric for customers. Plus, the store gave me a handsome discount on fabrics. So I sewed all my own clothes, which helped out my mom's budget tremendously. She needed every dime she had since Dad's alcoholism grew deeper and deeper.

My junior and senior years, I was never home much during the dinner hour, so I didn't have to do dishes anymore. Mom covered for me and lied to Dad about where I was, telling him I was at church or a church function.

In addition to working, I was a banner carrier and the practices also kept me away from home. Eight of us girls each held a letter that spelled our school name VALENCIA. We wore skimpy blue-velvet uniforms with scooped necks, a blue-ribbon choker around our throats, and yellow ruffled panties cut out

in back, with knee-high white vinyl lace-up boots—all our school colors, blue and gold. We were the Tigers. It was really something to get chosen to be a banner carrier and to march alongside the band in parades throughout California. Plus, we always brought home the gold in competitions.

My senior year, I began working at the Woof n' Warp fabric store in Costa Mesa, twenty minutes from home, located in the elite part of town, a village called South Coast Plaza. After I'd get off work, I'd rush home and make a new outfit for the next school day. It was my passion to make my own wardrobe. Having the power to choose my fabric and create beautiful stylish creations for myself empowered me. I never wore the same thing twice. I was voted best-dressed and the most likely to succeed. I was the Vice President for Future Business Leaders of America. I won several awards, none of which my parents watched me receive. They skipped my graduation as well. But my mentors Tanya and Freddie saw my achievements.

Dad was always drunk, and Mom was taking care of Phil, a fourth grader now, who had a penchant for burning things and playing with matches. We'd already had two close calls with him.

Phil also never got to experience a father as a decent role model. After I left home at eighteen, he and Dad were always beating up on each other.

Phil was trying to protect Mom, because she was Dad's main victim after I left home. Many times, I'd watched Dad almost kill her. If he wasn't choking her, he was slicing himself up by shoving his arm through our plate-glass window, thinking he'd been locked out.

Vern and Lorraine were long gone and I was barely there. Mom worked full-time, was nursemaid to Dad and my younger brother. Still, *she* was the one who allowed me to join the drill team, then on to being a banner carrier in the twelfth grade. She hated being home with my dad so she worked another five years for Sears in the catalog department in Hemet, California. She is the only reason our family survived. She was the bread winner and a very strong and determined woman.

Senior year was heaven to me. I had a lot of freedom. I was always traveling with our school band on Saturdays, in parades all over the area, bus rides to new and interesting places. I was even a member of the elite chamber music group of only six students out of our entire school. I loved to sing, and we were very good. I got to perform on stage, wearing a beautiful long, red formal gown that I made—that looked similar to the one Jennifer wore at the 86th Academy Awards in 2014, the year of the selfie with Ellen DeGeneres and Brad Pitt, when Jennifer won Best Actress for *Silver Linings Playbook*.

By now I knew who Jennifer Lawrence was. I knew she was Molly. My heart full with a mother's love, I traced my finger on the TV screen around her.

Jennifer has so much talent that she hasn't even tapped yet. She's going to shine more and more, if that's possible, because she's already fully equipped with everything she needs for success, including being one of her generation's greatest humanitarians.

CHAPTER FIVE

Unchaperoned Kegger Party
at Newport Beach

M OM WAS ON THE BRINK of a nervous breakdown. And I
didn't help.

My senior year in high school, 1973, my job at the Woof
n' Warp fabric store in Costa Mesa was practically a stone's
throw from Newport Beach, a very ritzy city for the wealthy.
So, obviously, for Spring Break, I rented an apartment in
Newport Beach and invited nine of my closest senior girlfriends to join me. We played Carol King music; the rumor
was she was dating James Taylor.

With my expertise at being a charmer, I had convinced
an old woman to rent me her house on the beach, under the
auspice that it was for my grandma and me to vacation. I also
convinced my Grandma P (my dad's mom) to sign the lease.
She had come to live with us this year, after my grandfather
socked her so hard in her eye that it detached her retina. He
ended up falling out the window at the Vine Street house in
Denver after the attack, he was so intoxicated from Jim
Beam. Two ambulances were called, one for her, one for him.
She survived, he didn't. He died a miserable, painful death.

At my beach-house party, all the girls had told their parents it was a chaperoned week at the beach with Bonnie's

grandma, except Grandma P wasn't really invited. She was my alibi. She would do anything to see her favorite granddaughter have some fun; after all, this was the first time I got to leave my yard, wink wink.

This party was the first event I ever hosted, not counting my sixteenth-birthday slumber party when I had talked Dad into *not* drinking that Friday night, and Mom made homemade pizzas while we girls played records, bobbed for apples, and decorated the garage with crepe- paper banners.

The beach-house party started out peaceful. My nine girlfriends and I could begin our initiation into freedom from our parents. It was our rite of passage. Each of us pitched in $10 for food and $50 for the rental. That gave me $500 to rent the house and $100 for food. I thought it would be plenty. I allowed each friend to invite one guest, giving us about twenty partiers. A nice size.

But word got out. An unchaperoned kegger party! Hundreds of young adults converged on the beach house.

When helicopters with spotlights flew overhead, I quickly left the party and drove the twenty miles to Grandma, in a panic. "Grandma! You've got to get in my car right now!"

"What's the matter? Why are you sweating, Bonnie?"

"You'd be sweating, too. Come on. Just get in and bring your purse. We're going to need it."

I piled my seventy-five-year-old grandma into my yellow mustang.

We got to the house after avoiding numerous road blocks. The police were already inside.

"Officer, what's the problem?" Grandma asked the tall uniformed officer holding a flashlight.

"Are you the adult renting this house?"

"Yes, I am, officer," she replied sweetly. "I hope you're going to remove all these uninvited people who are trying to crash our party."

"Yes, ma'am. We're trying to get the situation under control."

"Good. I'm tired and I want to go to bed."

And just like that, all the extra guests disappeared, just as quickly as they had converged.

Grandma made sure my nine girlfriends were all accounted for, then she turned to me. "Now take me home, Bonnie. I really have had a night of it."

I loved my grandma for that. No one got hurt, no arrests were made, but I know that every teenager age seventeen to nineteen who lived in Orange County went to our party that night. It was a party that went down in the history books. And I will always remember the authority I felt from coordinating all ten of us girls.

And at our Senior Prom—the Beach Boys played *live!* Hippies were the mainstay.

It was the wild wonderful 1970s.

PART II

Starting My Career As a Chef

(Love and Marriage)

CHAPTER SIX

My First Marriage

M Y SENIOR YEAR OF HIGH SCHOOL, the counselors made it very apparent that if I didn't enroll in college I would end up like my sister and my mom, getting married and having children at a young age. I didn't know I had a choice about where my life could lead, as I had been under my father's control my entire life.

After I graduated in 1973 from Valencia High School in Placentia, California, my life began to change. When I turned eighteen that fall, I was living with Mom and Dad and Phil in our Yorba Linda house; and Mom made me a deal, my only choice really, she said, if I wanted to succeed in life: "Bonnie I'll pay for your books so you can go to college, but you have to pay for everything else."

"Gee, Mom, that would be great! I have plenty to do with all the classes I can sign up for." I was grateful not to have to pay rent.

I majored in Fashion Design and Merchandising at California State Fullerton, our local college about fifteen minutes from home. I also enrolled in all the art classes I could, including Beginning Drawing, Color and Design. Purchasing my first pad of art pencils and bonded drawing paper was a dream come true! My entire life, I had longed to be creative but never had been allowed to express myself except through my economic sewing talent.

My freshman year, I met a guy named Joe. He, his best friend, and Tracy were going to a concert south in San Diego, the weekend before college classes started.

"It's Steely Dan, and a guy named Elton John. You've gotta go," Joe begged me to go with them.

"My parents will never let me go, Joe," I told him.

"Please ask your mom. It's going to be a really cool concert and I want you to see it."

"Oh, all right."

Joe and I were the same age. He was tall and good-looking, with the most enviable curly brown hair. He lived with his sister in Newport Beach next to Balboa Island, where John Wayne and his wife Pilar resided. It was a very posh part of town, on the ocean.

So that night I told my mom I was going with a girlfriend and, afterwards, spending the night at her apartment at the beach."

"You're eighteen," she said. "You can do anything you want now."

"What? I can go? Really? What about Dad? I won't get in trouble?"

"Just go," she said. "Your dad has no say over you anymore."

I immediately packed and was on my way. This was my liberation weekend!

I didn't come back until late Sunday night. Monday was the first day of college classes and I wanted to get a good night's rest.

Then I met Jim O'Leary. It was my first semester. My new best friend, Cindy Gould, who became a lifelong buddy, was in almost every class I was and we became inseparable. She was dating Steve, a young version of Robert Redford. And she introduced me to her boss, Jim O'Leary.

Jim was the manager at a sporting goods store at Fashion Island in Newport Beach. Although he was ten years older, we quickly fell in love.

Jim introduced me to a quality of life I soon would get used to. He lived on Lido Island, part of Balboa Island, both reserved for the very rich.

Jim had a big sailboat in the harbor. He drove a Porsche and took me all over. We skied in Utah; I was on my college ski team. We double-dated with Cindy and Steve.

When I first met Jim, I'd stand in front of the mirror in my bedroom at my parents' house—and pull and stretch on my eyes, trying to give myself wrinkles so I'd look older. With my baby face, ordering vodka gimlets was difficult. Though being with an older man, most of the time I wasn't carded.

Jim took me to the Sternwheeler almost every night, an actual sternwheeler ship renovated and refurbished, located on the water at Newport Beach, a fine-dining restaurant with a full bar. Sometimes, we went to the Quiet Woman or Victor Hugo's. It was all fine food.

Jim had all the toys. However, when he bought a Lamborghini, that didn't impress me. It was hard to climb into.

Then he found me my first apartment, on Balboa Island, and he paid for it. I kind of liked being a kept woman. This was a new-found life of luxury.

I loved that little upstairs apartment where I lived while going to college and had some of the best times of my life.

Then Jim introduced me to his very rich parents. They didn't seem to like the fact that I wasn't from money. They sure liked to brag a lot about all of their own accomplishments. I couldn't imagine having them as in-laws. Being rich meant nothing to me. I'd rather be happy. Jim's fast cars and extravagances were nice, but I didn't care for being looked down on when I went to dinner at their house.

So, I strayed.

I fell for someone else, someone who drove a Volkswagen. Enter Howard Lee Williamson from Orange, California.

It was my second year at college. I kept backing into his VW when exiting my apartment parking space on Balboa Island. I kept offering $20 for damages to his car and, eventually, we got to know each other.

We married six months later, on Valentine's Day 1975. Cindy Gould was my bridesmaid, and her boyfriend Steve Cobb was a groomsman. Howard's sister Joyce and my sister Lorraine were bridesmaids. We made all their white dresses, with red-embroidered hearts on the border. I made a dress for my niece Krissy, age three, Lorraine's daughter, even though Howard's niece was the flower girl. We had a huge multi-layered heart-shaped wedding cake, with fountains. It was a huge affair, a hundred-and-fifty guests at St. Joseph's Catholic Church across the street from my high school in Placentia.

I didn't want to go through with the marriage, after making the commitment—but Lorraine encouraged me. She was Matron of Honor. "Look at it this way," she said, "if it doesn't work out, you can always get divorced. Give it a try. You might like it."

I didn't realize then she wanted me to suffer, just like she was in her own marriage.

Shortly after the wedding, my dad sold the family home in Yorba Linda, where I had lived for ten years. Mom hated to leave that house. Years later, she told me it killed her spirit when Dad moved her into a shack at Lake Elsinore. Plus, they left behind the Chris Craft boat n' trailer in the garage, as they had no way to pull it.

Cindy and Steve remained my and Howard's best friends. They married a year later, and fulfilled their life destinies. She became an inhalation therapist for infants. He became a fireman. We started seeing less and less of them as our career choices led in different directions.

I was nineteen, and my husband was ten years older. We struggled financially, as he was beginning a career as a tool-and-die maker surviving the Vietnam war while suffering from PTSD and the effects of agent orange.

So, I stopped attending full-time college. I did allow myself one night class at Orange Coast Community College in Costa Mesa, needlepoint, which I dearly loved; sewing with yarn onto canvas rather than making garments.

Using my artistic talents, I also was a cosmetic instructor for Avon, working at Neiman Marcus at Fashion Island, where my once-boyfriend Jim had worked. Neiman Marcus was known for the finest quality items and couture fashion only for those with excess cash. The company gave me extensive training. Though I was not skilled enough for the fine-jewelry department, where they sold real diamonds, they allowed me to work the counter. I even learned to giftwrap packages by concealing the tape, an art itself.

Soon, I also became ensconced with the needlepoint craze that was exploding, and I made good money teaching classes and designing projects. That landed me a freelance job for a major needle-arts company, The Creative Circle in L.A., for whom I designed needlepoint kits and was paid almost a thousand dollars for my first kit.

Then The Artistic Needle, out of Fresno, launched its business and hired me as the Design Director. I designed hundreds of stitchery kits, in all mediums having to do with yarn. I also produced several catalogs and provided instructions for thousands of women across America. I was paid handsomely and put under exclusive contract, garnering $3,000 on my first royalties. I even rented our first house for Howard and me, which I filled with new and antique furniture. I got royalties for all the kits I designed, which were sold through direct marketing. Now, I could let go of my other freelance jobs, even though I continued working part-time at Neiman Marcus.

After three years of disillusionment with married life, now realizing I could support myself, I also realized I didn't want to be in a committed relationship anymore. So I separated myself emotionally from the marriage. It was only a sort of commitment anyway.

Howard was a Vietnam vet. He'd just gotten out of the service after four years of active duty. He was one of the first draftees in the sixties. He'd been to Asia, a place I'd never heard of. He had stories about the jungle and survival. I felt so sorry for him.

I hadn't known what good husband material looked like, so I had settled on this likeable, experienced world-traveler. But Howard drank a lot, just like my dad. Plus, he smoked pot, which I thought was a crime.

Then shortly after I turned twenty-one, Mom asked if my younger brother Phil, now fourteen, could live with Howard and me. She was in her fifties, with an alcoholic husband and constant fighting, and raising a teenager was just too much for her.

I agreed, thinking it would be an awesome opportunity for Phil to experience going to Corona del Mar High School at Newport Beach, a beach town where surfing was an actual Physical Education class and Phil wanted to learn how to surf.

Phil met his first love at that school. But when I caught him smoking pot with a friend behind the trash bin at our apartment complex, I sent him back to Lake Elsinore, to live with Mom and Dad.

Now looking back, I realize it was the worse decision I could have made for my younger brother. To this day, he still pines for his lost love. I was just too young and newly married.

Plus, having Phil live with us was the final dagger in our troubled marriage, as Howard himself was experiencing PTSD from his war experiences.

Even though I still struggled with low self-esteem and had thought my life was over at the big 2-0, I now realized I was beautiful.

Now twenty-two, I liked the attention men were showing me, and I started accepting compliments from men other than my husband.

That's when I met my Italian friend, Tony Rausa. He owned The Hair Factory in Costa Mesa, next door to the shop where I occasionally taught a needlepoint class.

My time with Tony was magical, even though he was forty years older. He was a man who really knew how to live.

Our relationship was innocent at first. I'd talk him into styling my hair. Soon, he was showing me what life was all about. He helped me leave my marriage and rent my own house in Costa Mesa. Every Monday, on his day off, he'd take me somewhere exciting.

It was 1979, the time of mini-skirts and go-go boots. We mingled with celebrities, constantly. We went to La Jolla and the Laguna Beach sawdust festival. We watched the Living Pageant of the Masters, actors motionless in recreated staged masterpiece paintings, like *The Last Supper*. We went to Los Angeles a lot, especially in the evening, where his daughter Patti was dating Denny Terio, a hot Italian dancer and the host of *Dance Fever*, sponsored by Merv Griffin. We danced to all hours of the night.

Sometimes we stayed over in Tony's expensive condo overlooking the Del Mar Race Track; and often mingled with Tony's neighbor, Willy Schumacher, the jockey.

All this while, I maintained my job at Neiman Marcus. Plus, I was making great money on royalties.

I was living the high life. So I thought.

CHAPTER SEVEN

My First Job As a Chef

THEN I MET ALLAN PERRY, and I was smitten. At twenty-four, I had divorced Howard and returned to college. I was in my element taking art classes. I was thriving.

Even with my employee discount at Neiman Marcus, I still made my own clothes. Plus, their clothes were either business leisure or fancy ball gowns, nothing in-between, nothing for someone like me.

I was drawn to Allan Perry like bees to the nectar from the moment I saw him. He wasn't strikingly handsome but he had the total package. A strong, brilliant man. He carried himself well, in his tight jeans, and was very charming, with the most beautiful smile I had ever seen. I was forever trapped in his big blue eyes.

"May I help you, sir?" I asked.

"I'm shopping for a blouse for my mother for Christmas," he said.

Wow, of course he was. I looked long and hard at him. He had now captured my undivided attention. Though he was twenty-two years older, I didn't see him as a father figure. It was all sexual energy.

He selected a golden silk blouse for his mom, sporting a $100 price tag.

I took the blouse to the back room to wrap the gift . . .

and hurriedly scribbled my phone number on my card: *If there are any other services you need, I am here for you,* signed Bonnie Williamson.

I had never been so brazen. I was visibly shaking. For the first time in my life, I trembled to my core.

(I did feel this soul-shaking thirty-five years later, the day I traced Jennifer's image on the TV screen with my finger, just as I was lamenting, *My soul knows who you are, Jennifer Lawrence, but my mind does not. Who are you to me?*)

I was still dating Tony, and I had just met Allan, when Tony took me on my first trip to New York City. We visited Macys and the FAO Schwartz toy company. Then we toured the entire East Coast and tasted the differences in cold-water vs. warm-water lobster in Newport, Rhode Island. Sampling the finest culinary delights opened up a whole new world to me.

But all I could think about was returning to California to hook up with Allan. He had gotten my note alright, and it didn't take long for him to initiate a full-time relationship with me.

Allan was a part of my destiny. We had a whirlwind romance, and I moved in with him soon. He had homes in Mission Viejo at Lake Finnestera, Laguna Hills, and a condo in Palm Springs, California.

And Allan loved my cooking! It had been a long time since he'd had someone cook homemade dinners for him.

I enjoyed my times in the kitchen with Allan by my side, as we sipped wine and listened to classical music. He was my prep cook, he did all the chopping. I created magnificent dinners, just for the two of us.

After dinner, we exclusively watched PBS on television. I was becoming cultured, I thought. Allan was soothing out my ruffled edges, I believed.

We did a lot of traveling. We went to Lake Tahoe, skiing. Flew in an airplane with Bill Clark and his younger wife, Bunny. Toured Taos, Santa Fe, Bryce National Park, The Arches, and Zion National Park. And stayed at my first bed-and-breakfast at the Domain Chandon property in Hearldsburg, Northern California.

Allan drove us in his shiny-black Cadillac touring car, with red pin-striping, which he'd earned as a used-car salesman. When I attended a needlework seminar in Albuquerque, sponsored by the Embroiders Guild of America, he picked me up in that car, with his two poodles in the back seat, Peter and Capricorn.

We smoked a lot of pot, too. Allan convinced me it would help my creativity as an artist. Pot did allow me to visualize colors and images with a completely unique perspective. But it did not help our sex life—and it is probably what started the onset of my COPD.

It was around that time, 1980, that I told Allan my parents were dead. I was embarrassed of them. They were commoners. I was better than they—and they were not welcome in my life anymore.

I disassociated myself from them. I did not call them. They would not approve of Allan and his age. They were still getting over the idea that, as a Catholic, I had divorced Howard. *So, to hell with them*, I had thought. They didn't deserve me.

Amazing how karma comes around, a lesson I had to learn. Be careful about what you ask for.

Today, in my sixties, with my daughter Jennifer (Molly) estranged from me, now for thirteen years, I am so ashamed that I ever denied my parents.

Our Restaurant

Allan had friends in Paso Robles, California, who had just secured a 99-year lease as an investment venture on a turn-of-the-century building with a mineral hot springs.

It was then that Allan convinced me that my cooking needed to be shared and enjoyed by others, not just him, and we formed a partnership. I became the chef and interior decorator. He provided the funding and became the host, for our restaurant: Perry's At the Hot Springs, in Paso Robles. We would split the profits, he promised.

I had just spent the last five years eating at fine restaurants, with Jim, then Tony, now Allan. I had learned to discriminate ingredients and had honed my taste buds, picking and choosing what got to enter my mouth. I had gained an incredible compendium of knowledge regarding foods. I was a self-taught cook. I knew what I liked and I had impeccable taste.

We traveled up and down the Northern Coast of California, mostly Carmel, as I carefully handpicked the restaurant's décor and fixtures. We ate at the best restaurants all along the coast, and I catalogued what I liked and what I thought would work in our own fine-dining restaurant.

This handsome turn-of-the-century building had good bone structure. It only needed my touch as an artist: One side would be a health resort, with the rejuvenating Sulphur waters. The other side a quaint yet state-of-the-art, out-of-the-way forty-seat restaurant.

I took an old 1950s mahogany buffet and cut holes in the top, turning it into a soup warmer, which was served by our waiters. I skinned the deli case with oak veneer and "brassed" all the metal parts, making it into a showcase for evening desserts.

I am a perfectionist, and I made our restaurant perfect, sparing no expense. I paid close attention to every detail. The remodel cost $100,000—of Allan's money.

I designed and drew all the menus and advertisements. I hired the staff and designed the uniforms I wanted them to wear. This wasn't just a restaurant, it was a finely honed performance. I only allowed men to serve at night, butler style. I contracted the vendors, prepared and cooked all the meals.

I insisted on only the finest and freshest ingredients in my kitchen. Seafood was trucked in daily from Morro Bay: abalone steaks, lobsters from Catalina Island, and only the finest grass-fed beef from Mavericks Ranch in Cholame, California, thirty-eight miles from the restaurant. All this was long before the finest up-and-coming vineyards, including Estrella, Robert Mondavi Domain Chandon, our house champagne.

One of my favorite dishes that I made was coa-quo-vin, an intricate chicken stew. I served the entrée in $40 chicken bowls that I had bought in my favorite gift shop in Carmel Valley. Most of them broke within a few washings, even when I asked for them to be hand-washed. I still have a complete set of those dishes in my home. I also retained my Hobart mixer, with which I made all the cheesecakes; as well as a few prints I had hung on the walls of the restaurant, mostly posters of French café scenes, except for one original French painting, "Motor Cycles Comio," of a French female with orange hair, riding a bike while chasing geese.

At our grand opening July 2, 1981, we had over five-hundred guests and everyone wore their finest. Live chamber music played in the background, and we offered a spread of hors d'oeuvres.

Famed Canadian singer-songwriter, Joni Mitchell, attended, though she mostly sat under the shade of one of the many oak trees that lined the river bank, because she wanted to just experience the beauty unfolding in this sleepy old town of Paso Robles.

Allan got caught up in operating an exclusive fine-dining restaurant and decided to have an unlisted phone number. To make a reservation in our "reservations only" restaurant, one had to be connected, as well as to get a reservation, and we were booked six months in advance.

We became the private little getaway for Quincy Jones and Peggy Lipton. We always had Quincy's favorite table available for him, up front next to the thirty-foot arched window that overlooked an expansive meadow. He would come in late in the evening, and we'd shut down the entire restaurant for his exclusivity, with a very special dinner prepared just by me. Then he would wander into the hot mineral baths, where we afforded visitors bottles of the finest Central Coast wines. Quincy Jones is a legend. Quincy is best known as a composer and record producer for legendary musicians, such as Frank Sinatra, Michael Jackson, Celine Dion, and Aretha Franklin.

As the full-time chef for this fine restaurant, I had to give up my career as design director for the Artistic Needle Company, so I no longer received dividends on all the hundreds of kits I had designed. Allan had put that kibosh in my contract. He didn't want me to have my own money.

He kept me as the chef at our restaurant as long as he could. I left the restaurant and ended our partnership in 1982, when I was twenty-seven. *And* he did *not* keep his bargain.

The only thing I ended up with was a lot of restaurant experience, room and board. Or should I say, bored.

Anyway, I was better off. I didn't want to be kept, after all. My parents had done a better job at that, I finally realized.

Besides, Allan had no intention of marrying me or having a family. As I was still a young woman, why should I be denied?

CHAPTER EIGHT

My Second Husband

In the winter of 1983, I met a cowboy named Jim while waitressing at a coffee shop. He shod horses for one of the Hearst family members, and we'd swim under the stars in the palatial pool at Hearst Castle. We were all friends when her cousin Patty Hearst joined the Lebanese Liberation movement and robbed a bank. I didn't know then that he had spent seven years in jail for murder.

I enjoyed their company very much—until he violently tried to strangle me to death, just as he had his wife Jane Eastman of the Kodak family, then forced me to an isolated house in Montana, all because I wanted to end the relationship.

I escaped by walking ten miles to a highway, where I hitchhiked to Santa Barbara. I called my parents and they picked me up and moved me to their boat docked in Dana Harbor.

I loved my life on that boat! Each morning, I trekked to the clubhouse to take a shower. I fished and caught my dinner . . . and cooked it right there.

I got a new boyfriend pretty quickly, a scuba diver who scrapped barnacles off the bottoms of boats. He, his friend Terry, and I would row out into the harbor in a dinghy and drink Gallo wine from a shared bottle under the full moon.

Terry was murdered shortly after. She was to meet me at my boat at midnight, after her singing set at the Green Lantern. When she didn't show up, I fell asleep. She was found the next morning, floating in the lagoon, her neck broken. She'd still been alive when someone pushed her off the pier and she sank.

Mom and Dad immediately moved me to Lake Elsinore and helped me to rent an apartment. I got a job as a waitress at a coffee shop. At night, I went to a local bar, Kay's, and danced up a storm.

Patrick worked for the Peace Corps with the Navajo Indians. He was a construction worker, very handsome, and a vibrant dancer We won several dance contests together.

His wife had recently passed He was about my age. I was done with older men. He was also an empath, like me, and extremely sensitive. I felt a synchronicity with him. Ours was a whirlwind romance, too.

A Spanish woman and her three sons hired me as chef for their Mexican restaurant, Café Laguna, on the lake. I taught Patrick the intricacies of cooking Mexican food: rellenos, tostadas, enchiladas. I had learned from my dad how to make green chili with fresh peppers.

St. Patrick's day, I got pregnant. A little too much Cervezas. Up above Lake Elsinore, Patrick wooed me under the moonlit sky and stars.

We moved back to Colorado, as both of us were natives. We married May 5, 1984, Cinco de Mayo, and offered a huge Mexican dinner for our guests. It was the first of many catered events.

I was sure I was pregnant with a girl, as I already knew I would have a girl named Molly. But, no. Sebastian Cody Vass was born December 14, 1984. As he was born I checked his body parts exclaiming "Molly, you're a boy!"

Cody was a joy for me. However, Patrick wasn't emotionally ready to be a father. Now that we were living at my family's cabin in Grand Lake, up in the mountains, his idea of supporting our family was to grow marijuana. I was glad my mom blatantly refused the grand idea. Though Patrick was thirty years ahead of his time. Marijuana was approved by voters in Colorado in 2012, legalized in January 2014.

When Cody was three months old, money was running out so I entered the May D & F "Whose Sauce Is Boss?" contest, judged by the *Denver Post* food editor Dick Kreck, KBPI radio's Alan Dumass, Channel 4's newsman Mark Grimm, and Channel 7's weatherman Ed Greene.

I won! My recipe "Bonnie's BOSS spaghetti sauce" merited me $500 and a set of Revere Ware cooking pans.

This gave me the confidence to apply for a job catering the City of Arvada's dinners for their various meetings, like the City Council and the Aging Committee. I was happy to commute the two hundred miles round trip ten times a month from the cabin to Arvada.

Patrick was studying for his real-estate certification, so my catering was our only source of income.

In July, I would catch rainbow trout from the lake out front and prepare a huge fish fry for the council members, serving twenty to thirty. I got such a good reputation for my food that soon I was catering for the likes of Colorado's Congressman, Dan Schaefer of the 6th district.

Patrick didn't pass his real-estate test and I was done with his illegal pot use, so I asked for a divorce. Cody was now seven months old.

At that, Patrick cut his wrists. I rushed him down the only road from Grand Lake to a doctor's office, in my grandma's 1963 Ford Fairlane, before he bled to death.

As we were leaving the doctor's, I told him, "That's it, Patrick. As soon as you're healed, I'm moving to Denver and getting a real job, making real money; get Cody and me an apartment—that has heat and hot water."

I was done.

To Bonnie, with appreciation for your fine
cooking and with gratitude for your many
kindnesses. Best wishes. Gerald R. Ford

CHAPTER NINE

Chef to a Retired President

THEN I SAW AN AD IN THE *Rocky Mountain News*: "Wanted. Personal Chef. Would you like to live in a prestigious home, drive beautiful cars and travel, while preparing meals for a couple? Send your resume to XYZ, Denver CO."

That's exactly what I wanted to do! So, I went to the library and typed a resume. I'd never had a resume before and I didn't know the first thing about designing one. I just did my best and got it in the mail ASAP.

Very soon after, I got a call. And nothing I would ever have expected.

"Hello, is this Bonnie Vass?"

"Yes. Who's calling?" I said, hoping it wasn't a bill collector.

"This is Ann Cullen from President Ford's office."

"Are you sure you have the right number?" I asked.

"Yes, I'm sure," she said.

"Umm, President Ford? Is that like the Ford Motor Company?"

She giggled. "No. President Ford, as in former President of the United States, retired Gerald R. Ford."

Now I knew she had the wrong phone number. "What is it you want?" I asked, expecting her to ask for a donation for the Republicans or something.

"Mrs. Ford would like to interview you for the job you applied to recently."

I knew I was in trouble.

"You recently sent your resume to a blind ad in Denver, right?"

"Well, yes, I did."

"Well, Mrs. Ford and the President liked what they saw and she'd like to you drive to Beaver Creek next Sunday, September the 19th."

"That's my birthday," I said. My thirtieth birthday.

"Yes, we know, but it's the only day they can fit you into the President's schedule."

"Is this a joke?" I asked.

"No, I assure you. It's quite legitimate. Look, I'll mail the date and time and where to show up. Just check in at the guard gate as you approach the hill. See you then." And she hung up.

As I hadn't left Patrick yet, he asked, "Who was on the phone?"

"President Ford's office. I have a job interview from the resume I sent last week."

"Really? He's a Republican. I can't wait to tell my mother. She's been heading the Republican group in Littleton for years."

I drove down the mountain from our cabin in Grand Lake to Denver to buy something new to wear, using money I had saved from my catering work and from the cooking contest I'd won.

What do you wear to meet a President? I wondered.

I decided on an off-white skirt with a red-and-blue check pattern. Teamed with my red-silk Neiman Marcus blouse with a bow, it was perfect. I bought a pair of white hose and conservative navy-blue pumps.

This had better work, I told myself, as I had used the last of my savings.

I knew the dream job would be short-lived once they realized I wasn't qualified, but it was the only chance I'd have to meet President Ford and Betty Ford.

I dressed at Patrick's mom's house in Littleton, so I could have a hot shower before I left for the interview back up the hill, and I borrowed her nicer, more reliable car.

Good thing I did. On the way back up the mountain to Beaver Creek, near Vail, I got stuck in a freak snowstorm at the base of the Eisenhower Tunnel, thirty-five curvy mountain miles from my destination.

It was advised to chain up—but I certainly wasn't going to chain up in my new fancy skirt, white stockings, and dress pumps. So, I forged ahead, slowly, noticing several cars sliding into the ditch.

I finally made it to the Fords' guard gate, an hour-and-a-half late.

"Will they still see me?" I asked the guard. "I got stuck in a terrible snow storm." On and on I went.

"We know. Yes, they're waiting for you."

I was a bundle of nerves. I was in no shape to meet anyone, let alone a former President of the United States.

Ann Cullen, Mrs. Ford's personal assistant, greeted me at the door. Snow was flying everywhere. My hair, once nicely coiffed, was in disarray and I was freezing. I hadn't worn a blazer. *Strike one,* I thought.

Ann was kind. Seeing my panic, she pointed to a door. "The ladies room is that way. Go take a deep breath and gather yourself. Mrs. Ford will meet you in the next room shortly."

I passed rows and rows of brand-new skis, boots, and a vast array of snow outfits, in every color and size imaginable. The downstairs looked like a ski shop.

Bonnie, I thought to myself, *you'd better take it all in. Once they find out you're unqualified, you'll never be back.*

After making myself presentable, I found the room with the massive fireplace and roaring fire. I sat on the white sofa, at attention, and waited.

Ann entered, with Betty Ford, and said, "Mrs. Ford, let me present Bonnie Vass."

I jumped to my feet and stuck out my hand in a greeting. "Betty, it's such an honor to meet you!" I said enthusiastically. I didn't know if I was supposed to bow or courtesy, too.

She reluctantly shook my outstretched hand. "Please remain seated."

I rubbed my sweaty palms on the white sofa.

"I like your accomplishments in life thus far," she said. "The President and I have decided to hire you as our new chef."

"I . . . I . . . I really don't know much about fine cooking, ma'am."

"I know," she said. "The President prefers simple, clean food. We require lunch to be a salad, with homemade dressing, nothing bottled. Same for dinner, but not a meal, as in lunch. Plus, we have to have dessert at both meals. But no sugar must ever be used in the home."

"Can I use a substitute?"

"Yes, of course. Think you can handle that?"

I nodded.

"The dinner entrée will be from a recipe card I will give you. His favorite is crowned meatloaf. Have you ever made that?"

I shook my head. "No."

"I expected not. I will guide you. Two vegetables at dinner with the entrée, then dessert in the den with coffee. A refrigerated cookie is fine on occasion for lunch. I'll give you the recipe for Sandies." She rose from the wingback chair. "You were so late getting here that the President had to head out with the Secret Service to catch his flight, but we've already done the background check on you and your family."

Oh, my God. . . But we passed.

"On one condition," she said. "Never again will you call me Betty. My name is Mrs. Ford." She looked down her nose sternly toward me. "And your husband will be my husband's valet."

"Oh, that's impossible. We're getting a divorce. He has to stay home and watch our baby."

"We have two bedrooms in the maids' quarters. He can have one, you the other. Your son will stay with your parents when we're in California, and his parents when we're in Colorado. End of discussion," she said and turned.

"Can't I keep him with us?" I begged.

"No allowances will be made. You can visit him on Sunday afternoons during your time off."

"Please, Mrs. Ford, do we have to live with you?"

"Do you want the job?" She knew I needed the job. "Any questions?"

"How much does the position pay?"

"$1,000 a month. Plus room and board."

"Do we get to eat what you do?"

"Sometimes." She headed to the door. "We will see you in Palm Springs in two weeks. Ann will provide expense money for you." And she walked out.

I stood there motionless. $1,000 a month for the *both* of us, and I could see Cody only *once* a week? I shook my head. What had just happened?

I just got hired to be President and Mrs. Ford's chef, that's what happened.

Patrick and I worked six days a week, eleven to twelve hours a day, half days on Sundays. I was also *on call* at night, from my personal bedroom on the premises, in case a button

fell off Mrs. Ford's bed coat and she'd have me sew the button back on.

Plus, I wasn't allowed to drive more than *twenty* miles at any given time in their town car, not having my own vehicle while here. This eliminated trips to my parents to visit Cody, because it was over a hundred miles one way.

That job is how I gained a keen understanding of how a person can become brainwashed, as Molly would be against me when she was a teen.

Mrs. Ford had just recently given up alcohol and she exhibited all the signs of a "dry drunk." It's the same nasty behavior as when you're drinking—but you're not but you wish you were. Her problem went even deeper, because she combined barbiturates with the alcohol, which made her dopey as well.

And she took it out on the ones closest to her, me and Patrick. She knew we weren't going anywhere.

Patrick's job was to have the President's breakfast ready for him at seven a.m. It consisted of freshly squeezed orange juice from the trees by the pool, a fresh fruit cup, and a piece of dry wheat toast or a bowl of wheat germ or bran flakes.

Mrs. Ford required coffee at nine a.m., sometimes a piece of wheat toast, but sugarless jam had to be available if she so fancied. She required lunch promptly at twelve noon. It consisted of a salad with a protein and homemade salad dressing, no sugar or oil added. Sometimes, she wanted a piece of lavash, low-fat flavorless cracker rounds, and fresh sun tea with a couple of refrigerator cookies, again no sugar.

Dinner started with a small vegetable salad, no sugar or oil in the dressing. The entrée was a protein of grilled chicken, orange roughy, or an occasional crowned meatloaf, with two vegetables steamed or baked. Steaks were served only when we had guests for dinner. I made a lot of sorbets and sherbets for desserts; and I never used white flour, sugar, or fat of any kind. It was a healthy way to eat and kept them both fit and trim. That diet is the reason they both lived long lives, the President to ninety-three, Mrs. Ford five years further.

After a while, I asked her for a raise for us or Patrick would have to leave, and she said, "You are ungrateful. Your rewards in the future will come from your experience here. That should be sufficient. You don't need anything other than what we are providing to you."

"But I need to be with my son. We never get to spend time with him, and he's only a baby once. Please," I pleaded, "let him join us in the back room."

"No," she said and slammed her fist down onto the desk. The President doesn't have any grandsons and I will not have him getting attached to yours. He is not worthy."

This took me aback.

Patrick quit after only a couple of months, so he could stay with our baby—but he quit in a most inappropriate way. The Canadian Edmonton Oilers' hockey team were coming that night for hors d'oeuvres and drinks, leaving me without a butler to serve. I asked Mrs. Ford if I could ask my former restaurant partner Allan to come since we were in a bind. She couldn't get anyone from the LA agency; she had a bad reputation for the way she had treated help and she was notoriously cheap. Allan arrived in time to greet the guests, and I provided a lavish spread for the hockey team.

Finally, after nine months, through the fall and winter, I too had had enough and, at the end of June 1986, I left.

Though through 1987, whenever a newly hired chef couldn't make it in, Mrs. Ford sent the Secret Service to get me at King Soopers in Denver. I finally told my boss, "I'll quit if you make me go up the mountain one more time!"

I later received an award from the Secret Service agents for being the longest-lasting chef Mrs. Ford was able to keep.

As I had no vehicle after leaving the Fords, Mom and Dad picked me up and drove me to the cabin at Grand Lake. Dad tried to fix me up with Patrick again, but I was done with him. I needed a man who was able to support his family.

Mom and Dad also helped me to buy the white Jeep Wagoner in which I had delivered meals to the City of Arvada, because I convinced the City to reinstate my catering contract. They were glad to have me back.

That was when Patrick realized I was serious about leaving him.

I let him remain at the cabin. In turn, he took care of Cody, whom he loved very much.

My catering business gave me money to move. I would no longer stay at the cabin, which had no heat. I'd had my share of heating the house by fireplace as well as one too many lean years. I was a smart woman, young and capable.

CHAPTER TEN

Jennifer's Father

I WENT TO THE *Denver Post*, searching for a job. Again, I answered a classified ad: "A professional couple seeking a personal chef who can do some light housekeeping as well." I made sure I got the job.

I gave Patrick my catering business as a peace offering, as well as the majority of my money to use for catering supplies and caring for Cody. I did not ask him for support. Realizing his gravy train was over, he got an apartment in Denver, and almost immediately married his neighbor, a single mom with two young children, a new wife to take care of him.

My new job as a personal chef was in the "Old Money" part of Denver. The house I worked and lived in was a two-story Georgian with large white columns in front, five bedrooms, several baths, and a full basement. They had a gardener, a housekeeper, and now me. They let me stay in their son's bedroom, as he didn't live there anymore. Barbara was the head designer and her husband, Victor, the owner of their business, Victor Huff and Associates, a design firm that decorated and designed hotel rooms and lobbies. Their house even looked like a hotel.

The Huffs got a kick out of it whenever I filled in for the maid, because I left my signature mark with the toilet tissue by folding the corners back in a "V" shape, for Victor. They liked me to wear a French maid's outfit when I cleaned, with white stockings; a white chef's coat and hat when I served dinner. I obliged. It kept my street clothes clean. It was all a charade, anyway, dressing up, being someone different, like acting.

They weren't a happy couple. He was much older; she was a "trophy wife." So if dressing up cheered them, I played the part.

Then Barbara took on the role of matchmaker. She bragged about me to one of their designers at their firm, Mr. JJ William Brown, III, telling him how I had been the personal chef for former President and Mrs. Ford during their retirement, and that I'd had my own Country French restaurant in Northern California in wine country next to the Hearst Castle, and I was now their employee.

JJ was a gifted designer with a degree in architecture, and spent most of his free time fishing. He lived to fish, Barbara told me. It was all he talked about, she said, that and going to church on Sundays.

Several times I heard her talking about her golden boy to Victor at dinner or during conversations in the study. She seemed to have a crush on JJ. He was more her age.

Late one day, she said to me, "Bonnie, we need to have a special dinner tonight. Let's do a fish entree for the main course. A colleague just showed up in town and we want him to have a nice meal, casual but elegant."

I needed to pick up the pace. I hadn't cleaned the bathrooms yet, as it was the housekeeper's day off, and dinner was in three hours. I rushed to a specialty market at Colorado Boulevard and Hampden, where I bought the freshest red snapper.

For dinner, I wrapped the fillets around three sprigs of bright-green summer asparagus and simmered it al dente in a fresh tomato remoulade, made with garlic and herbs fresh from their garden. I paired this with Near East rice pilaf, my staple starch, plus a bit of fresh lemon. I added a butter lettuce salad with red onion slices, mandarin orange, and a poppy-seed dressing made from scratch, from the recipe Mrs. Ford had given me. I already had my famous New York-style cheesecake on hand, as it was the Huffs' favorite dessert. I served it with a fresh berry puréed compote on top.

Then I heard the light clinging of their dinner bell. I entered the dining room with the salads. As I slid the salad plate in front of their guest, his eyes met mine and I heard angels sing, I swear. Time stopped. No one else existed. I didn't even realize he had dropped his fork. Barbara was saying something.

"Let me get you a fresh one, Mr. Brown, I gushed."

I rushed to the kitchen, his fork in my hand, out of breath, and stood back against the dining-room door. The infamous JJ William Brown the third, and I was holding his fork.

I was still married to Patrick. I did not want a new boyfriend, or a husband. I was sworn off men. I already was a two-time loser.

Thoughts rushed through my mind. The first marriage didn't count, I'd been only nineteen.

I listened through the door.

Mr. Brown said, "You were right, Barbara. She is quite a looker."

I blushed.

When I returned to clear the plates at the end of the meal, Mr. Brown gently grabbed my arm and asked me, "What was that, red snapper remoulade?"

I almost fainted. He was touching me, talking to me.

"Yes, Mr. Brown."

"Oh, call me JJ. I will order that the next time I go out to eat."

"You'll never find that at a local restaurant," I blurted. "I'll just have to make it again for you sometime." Then I rushed out of the room, dirty dishes in hand, my mind swirling. I knew I was going to get fired.

I was just about done handwashing the china when in walked Mr. Brown. I avoided his gaze and starred straight into the sink.

He grabbed a towel and whispered into my ear, "Is this the one Barbara uses to dry the dishes?"

Nervous, I turned my head slightly. "Uh, huh."

"Barbara tells me you love to fish."

Now that was one subject that brought me out of my shell, and we talked about fishing until we'd dried and put away all the dishes.

When he left the kitchen, he said, "Nice chatting with you, Bonnie."

"Likewise, Mr. Brown."

"JJ," he corrected.

Later on that evening, I was sweeping the kitchen floor when JJ burst back in and grabbed me square by the shoulders. "You're my lucky charm."

I looked at him in utter shock. "What?"

"I just drove to the gas station and bought a lottery ticket. I felt lucky after meeting you. I not only won a hundred bucks on a scratch-off, but I feel like I won the lottery in more ways than one, meeting you tonight." He leaned in and kissed me softly on the cheek.

Immediately after meeting JJ, he encouraged me to get my own place. He didn't want to date me while I was living at his boss's house. Being the people pleaser I was, I found an apartment.

My small apartment in Cherry Creek on Colorado Boulevard was the most awesome apartment I'd ever had. Though one bedroom and one bath, it had a full kitchen with a small dining area set in an alcove. The living room had a fireplace.

The 1920s building was a converted estate with multiple floors, and housed four couples. I made a deal with the owner to shovel the walkways when it snowed and he deducted $50 off my rent. When it wasn't snowing, I cleaned the laundry common area outside my kitchen door and kept the sidewalks swept. This made my rent only $300.

In an alley, I found two twin-bunkbeds with mattresses. They were 1950s cowboy chic, with half a wagon wheel on top, half at the bottom. They fit perfectly in the small bedroom, one bed for me, one for Cody. I felt like I was home.

And that's where JJ and I shared our first intimate dinner together.

I also quit my job at the Huffs and got a better-paying union job at King Soopers' grocery chain. As their Specialty Meat Chef, I designed "grab-and-go" meals for hungry customers needing a quick dinner.

I also packaged my own personal brand of meals in individual tins, like TV dinners for singles, using all fresh ingredients and my secret recipes I had developed over the years. I called these "bachelor dinners" and peddled them to the mom-and-pop markets off Broadway Street near downtown Denver.

King Soopers was impressed and asked me to produce a line of meals just for *them*, like my own, to sell in their stores. I got a lot of enjoyment experimenting while creating their entire line of uncooked prepared meals for the public. Those "single" meals were an enormous success, and *all* the King Soopers grabbed onto my new line, then expanded to all the Krogers/Fred Meyers throughout the entire U.S.

Pre-Nups

January 1987, Cody and I moved in with JJ in his historic Hancock district Victorian home near Cherry Creek, which he had remodeled.

On Valentine's Day, as I was cleaning carrots under the faucet, below the stained-glass window in the kitchen, he nuzzled my earlobe, pulled me close and slowly kissed the nape of my neck, his hairy chest jetting out from under his white V-neck cotton shirt.

"B, I want you to marry me. I want to grow old with you forever. Will you have me? I know this is sudden, but I've been looking for you for a long time. It's right. It's time. I want you as my wife."

I turned to him, his hands on my shoulders. "I've been praying for this, J. I love you with all my heart. YES."

We embraced and I cried tears of joy.

After we put Cody to bed and read him a story, a guest arrived, a store owner presenting us with a large case filled with diamonds in all shapes and sizes. JJ chose for me a two-carat heart-shaped diamond with impeccable clarity.

Afterwards, he had it made into a small pounded gold band with the heart diamond perched on top ever so nicely.

In late 1988, I moved with JJ from Denver to Portland, Oregon. The Red Lions Hotels and Inns corporate office in Vancouver, Washington had hired him to be their lead architect. I landed my dream job as Catering Manager at the 500-room Red Lion Lloyd center in downtown Portland.

JJ and I lived alone in an upscale one-bedroom two-story loft on Jantzen Beach island, overlooking the Columbia River. He'd made arrangements with Patrick to care for Cody for six months during our transition to the Pacific North West.

"Cody and Patrick are such good buddies," JJ told me. "We'll fly Cody here for the holidays. You'll still have full custody. Patrick is just acting as caregiver, and we'll pay him."

It was the hardest thing I ever did, leaving my baby boy as I embarked on a new life, but I trusted JJ's judgment.

From the moment we arrived, I began planning for Cody to join us in six months. However, when it came to time to bring him to Oregon, as promised, JJ dragged his feet.

I wasn't seeing a future with JJ if Cody wasn't by my side. JJ didn't believe I would choose my child over him. But I did. When the six months was up, I moved.

I rented a small two-bedroom house next to Aunty Pat, as Cody called her. The General Manager's personal assistant at my job, Pat helped me. Plus, I enrolled Cody in a pre-school next to our office in downtown Portland.

In June 1990, after a visit from my mom, who now lived in California, I asked JJ to my office for a heart-to-heart. He was still upset that I had gone against his demands.

"JJ, we've been engaged over three years. We've lived together five. I've been getting offers from eligible bachelors, so I am returning your ring."

Visibly shaken, he said. "You can't do that."

"Really?"

He stood and rubbed his jaw as if he'd been slapped. "Well, okay, if you can get our old pastor Danny Daniels from back in Colorado to marry us, I'll do it," he conceded.

"Do what?" I asked, hiding a smile.

"I . . . I . . . I'll marry you." He kicked his foot at the floor.
. "Great. I'll take care of all the wedding arrangements. You just have to show up."

I moved fast, before he would change his mind. He had just turned forty-four, a confirmed bachelor. I would be thirty-five in September.

I should have walked, but I wanted a daddy for Molly—whom I *knew* would be born, soon. In fact, I knew seven years *before* I even met JJ.

I contacted the minister Danny and scheduled the wedding ceremony to be performed at Grand Lake, Colorado during the Fourth of July weekend, which gave both JJ and me extra days off our jobs. I then called JJ back and relayed that we would be married in one month.

"You better be worth it," he said.

CHAPTER ELEVEN

Nightmare Honeymoon

OUR PERSONAL CEREMONY WAS LOVELY on the pier at the glacial Grand Lake, overlooking Mt. Baldy.

"I will always protect and honor you," he said to me in his vows.

"I will always cherish you, with enduring love," I responded.

Our only guests were JJ's brother as best man, his wife Eve as my attendant, our minister Danny and his wife.

Bill and Lorraine, who owned Budget Tackle where JJ and I had bought all our fishing tackle for several years, crashed the wedding. They hid behind a tree as we said our vows, then popped out when we were walking down the trail to the car. I hurriedly added two more dinner guests at the Ruby's Red Fox Inn.

It was a beautiful summer night when JJ and I retired to our Honeymoon Suite overlooking a vast forested meadow alongside Winding River.

We had agreed to no sex for the previous month to make this night more special. I was ready, at my peak physically, in my best shape ever at 119 pounds, plus I had been jogging for three years.

I also was taking vitamins to get pregnant, for Molly, even though JJ made us use two kinds of birth control. He

71

did not want any kind of pregnancy. He had made that very clear: NO CHILDREN.

His brother had the same mantra: No children, ever. He had made his own wife Eve get her tubes tied *before* he would marry her, and hinted that I should do the same.

I would never do that, *knowing* that God was going to give me Molly.

In our honeymoon suite at Winding River Ranch, JJ and I had a little wine with dinner. Afterwards, I was looking forward to consummating our wedding vows. I came out of the bathroom in my new satin peach-negligee. I looked scrumptious and I was ready to make mad passionate love.

But JJ was in his underwear on the bed, rocking back and forth in the fetal position, bawling his eyes out. "What have I done?" he cried.

I went to the bathroom to get tissues for him. When I came back, he had slipped into bed and turned away from me.

I sat on the bed. "JJ, honey, what's the matter?"

"Shut off the light. Goodnight ," he said tersely and threw me an air kiss.

Stunned, I gripped wadded Kleenexes as I cried myself to sleep.

The next morning, JJ's brother BIL and his wife Eve were waiting for us at mom's cabin. They had just gone for a swim in Grand Lake. "C'mon, let's go for a hike," BIL said.

I was still in shock from the honeymoon night. "Okay," JJ said energetically and off we went, taking no water or food. I followed.

We hiked and hiked and hiked, twenty-two miles, over rough terrain.

My in-laws were athletic. Their idea of a good time was a thirty-five mile triathlon.

"J, when are we going to turn around?" I asked, as we continued to climb in elevation.

"Soon."

But we didn't. We walked all the way to the end of Granby Reservoir and over the dam.

At the dam, I said, "J, I can't go another step. How are we getting back?" I had huge bleeding blisters on my heels. I wasn't wearing the right kind of shoes for this torture, and it was another seven miles back.

JJ walked over to his brother. "Hey, man, she's not going any further."

"No problem. We'll run back to the cabin, pick up the car, and come back for you."

JJ was tired as well, though he wouldn't admit it.

While we waited for the car, I just sat there, in shock.

"I promise, we'll live happily ever after, you, me and Cody," JJ said. "I'll build us a log home on Salmon Creek in Vancouver, Washington."

We spent the rest of our honeymoon at my family's cabin in Grand Lake—where I did conceive Molly.

CHAPTER TWELVE

My Five-Year-Old Attacked by Wolves

A S CODY WAS ONLY FIVE, he had stayed with Patrick during our honeymoon. Patrick was now in Fallbrook, California, managing a forty-acre avocado ranch.

I was gratefully back at work from the awful honeymoon, at my job in downtown Portland, and Cody was still with Patrick for a time.

My secretary Marlene stood nervously before me.

"What's up?" I asked.

She furrowed her brow. "Dennis needs you in his office, right now."

"Uh-oh. Am I getting fired?"

"No."

My boss's face was flushed. He blotted sweat from his forehead. "Bonnie, sit down." He hesitated. "I don't know how to tell you this, Bonnie." He paused. "Your son has been in a terrible accident . . . and they don't expect him to make it."

"What?" I collapsed in a chair and broke into tears. "What happened?"

"He was attacked by a pack of wolves. They flight-lifted him to San Diego Children's Hospital. JJ is waiting for you at the airport. Your mom is on her way there, too."

"Oh, my God!"

"Marlene will take you to your apartment so you can pack. Then she'll take you to the airport. The plane leaves in two hours. Here's $200 for incidentals."

I ran out of the office, mascara streaming down my face. As Marlene drove me to my apartment, I asked, "How could this happen?"

I grabbed a duffle bag, toiletries, and we were off. She dropped me at the United Airlines check-in and handed me my ticket. "I'll meet you inside," she said and went to park.

She joined me inside at the line and warmly embraced me.

Frazzled, I endured the two-hour flight to San Diego, my eyes red and puffy. By six p.m., I hadn't eaten breakfast or lunch, and it didn't help that I got pregnant on our honeymoon, which only I knew. I hadn't told JJ. He'd want me to get an abortion and I was eight weeks pregnant.

When we would land soon, I ran to the bathroom, nauseous, and splashed water on my face.

The plane landed at twilight. Mom and JJ were waiting and I ran into his arms. "Is he still alive?" I asked.

He nodded. "He's stabilized."

I sighed. The guardian angels were with Cody.

JJ hurried me. "They're waiting for us to do surgery. They need *your* permission."

I looked around. "Where's Patrick?"

"No one knows," Mom said in exasperation.

This was the first time I'd seen her since Dad passed in 1988.

I stood outside Cody's hospital room, the monitor going beep, beep, beep. Shaking and crying, I tried to push the nurse out of my way, to get to my baby. He was only five and I hadn't seen him in two months. "Is he dead?" I asked her frantically.

She smiled comfortingly. "He's hanging in there." She took me to another room.

"A pack of wolves?"

"He was outside playing catch with a dog that was in heat, and a very large white wolf ran up to him from the orchard and bit the left side of his face, broke his jaw, and plunged him to the ground. Cody tried to get away, holding his arm over his face, but the wolf clenched his arm, almost detaching it. The dog tried to protect Cody," she said comfortingly.

"My baby!"

I ran for his room but she pulled me back. "I must tell you what to expect."

"No, no." I shook my head and slumped back onto the couch.

"The animal protection agency is scouring the canyon, looking for the wolf. They think one of the men wounded it. It *must* be found alive with its brain intact to find out if it has rabies. If the wolf isn't found, after the surgeries we have to start immediate injections."

That's when I lost consciousness.

I woke to smelling salts and sat up on the couch.

"You fainted." She patted my hand.

"What's next?" I asked forlornly.

"A team of neurosurgeons will reattach the ligaments in his face. We won't know the extent of the nerve damage until they operate. Afterwards, another team will reattach his arm, if they can save it."

"Please, please, please. Can I go see him now?"

She nodded. "I just needed to prepare you."

I entered the room slowly, and gently touched Cody's arm. "Mommy's here, honey."

His closed eyelids fluttered. He was in an induced coma but I felt he knew I was there.

His right arm was heavily bandaged from the elbow up, held in place by a stint. A gauze bandage was fastened around his face and covered both ears. I could see his eyes and little nose.

Another nurse entered and unwrapped the bandages from around his head. "Brace yourself," she warned.

Just as she said that, I saw Cody's left cheek fall into the bandage. I could see his teeth and the jagged tear where the wolf had tried to eat off his face and had taken most of his left ear as well. My poor little man.

I left the room, feeling helpless and a failure. How could I have let this happen?

The surgeons attached his arm that night and sewed his face back on. JJ, Mom, and I sat in the waiting room, praying until the wee hours of the morning. *Please spare my child.* I had never prayed so hard in my life.

Earlier, JJ had called Danny and asked him to gather up all the prayer warriors in Denver to pray for the surgeons' hands to guide them and to show them how to restore my son and make him whole again.

Patrick showed up several hours later the next day.

He'd left the orchard early the day of the attack to deliver a load not of avocados—but of marijuana!

He'd left Cody with the husband and wife caretakers who lived on the property. They were getting their own two kids ready for school and kept telling Cody, "Go outside and play with the dog."

They had sent him out of the house several times. She scolded him and sent him back out. "I told you, don't come back in until I tell you!"

When she heard the loud commotion, one of her children called to her. "Mom! Come quick!"

She ran to the door and saw Cody crawling with his good arm, as the dog was trying to keep the wolf off him.

She told a worker to call Flight for Life and to meet her *fifteen miles up the road* to pick up the badly injured child.

She scooped my son's face and arm into her t-shirt and, with her husband and kids, drove Cody to the top of the hill where a helicopter was waiting. It was a hundred miles to the hospital.

They and Patrick had known there were wolves on the property—and they didn't feed them. They wanted them hungry. And she had known they were there. These wolves were allowed at the perimeter to keep poachers from stealing the marijuana, which was masked by the avocado trees.

Patrick was not farming avocados. He was a pot farmer.

He begged me not to sue his boss, who had threatened that he would lose his job.

But who was going to pay the hospital bills? And what about Cody's long recovery? What kind of lifetime treatment would he need? I needed to restore Cody's quality of life.

Cody did indeed need several surgeries over many, many years. He lost the hearing in his left ear. His face was slightly drooped and he'd lost his salivary glands, so he couldn't retain saliva in his mouth and he constantly had to slurp in his drool. He also had PTSD and needed specialized care. He was constantly looking over his shoulder, fearing something would attack him from behind.

Patrick continued to wreak havoc.

Still to this day, he lies to our son, convincing him that *I* made Patrick lose his job and that's why Patrick's life never amounted to anything. He convinced Cody that I was his enemy.

Patrick even lied to the State of California and had Cody transported by federal officers back to California *after* JJ, Cody and I had moved into our log house in Vancouver, Washington.

Patrick has been absent ever since.

I hired Attorney John O'Brien in Santa Ana, a friend of Allan Perry's. John took my case pro-bono. I sued the owner of the "avocado ranch" and won the first-ever monetary award for a canine biting.

I call it the Cody Award. That's why, now, when people apply for homeowner's insurance, they are asked if they have any wild animals or specific types of dogs.

Cody was awarded several million dollars, which is being dispersed to him over the length of his life, up until he is age forty in 2024, when he will receive his final payout.

I also started a foundation, "Mothers Against Bad Dogs" (MABD), to support parents with counseling, advice, and comfort for their children.

Cody still gets the checks I won for him in court, but he hasn't spoken to me for many years.

CHAPTER THIRTEEN

Unwanted Pregnancy

T HE DOCTORS SEWED my little guy back together. He also had to suffer through the agonizing rabies' shots for twenty-one days. One of the trackers had shot the wolf dead.

Still in the waiting room, I whispered to JJ, "J, I have something to tell you."

"What?"

"I took a pregnancy test today. It's positive."

"Positive for what?"

"We're pregnant."

He jumped up. "Whose is it?"

"Well, it's yours."

"I haven't been home long enough! I've been in San Diego!"

I took his arm reassuringly. "J, it only takes one time to get pregnant."

"I know it's not mine! Get another test!" he shouted and stormed away.

"He's just under a lot of stress," Mom said, "with his grand opening coming up."

"He's still getting used to being a husband," I said, trying to defend him, as I held my face in my hands.

Later that day, JJ walked into Cody's room and threw a small plastic bag at me. "Here, try this. And this time, I'm going to watch."

I opened the bag. A pregnancy test.

"And if this one doesn't work!" he shouted, "I've arranged a blood test for you!"

Mom turned her head away, trying to distract Cody from the conversation, as he was now awake.

"What is it Daddy J?" five-year-old Cody asked. "Is it a present for me?"

"No, son. It's something for your mommy."

"Come on," JJ demanded and pulled me to the small bathroom. "Get in there. I'm on my lunch break. Let's get this over with!"

After removing the soiled stick, I said, "Happy now?"

With authority, he put the stick into the plastic bag and left Cody's hospital room, muttering, "There'll be no tampering with this one."

I didn't go back to the hotel that night with my mom.

JJ woke me the next morning, as I lay slumped asleep beside my baby's hospital bed. He shook my arm and poked at me. "Wake up. I made arrangements with a nurse for you to take a blood test. If you really are pregnant, we can find out who the father is."

I rubbed my eyes. "What? You've got to be kidding."

"No, I'm as serious as your dad's heart attack."

I jumped up, ran into the bathroom, and heaved out my guts. "There. Is morning sickness enough proof for you?"

"I don't give a damn about you throwing up. I just want to know I'm not the father."

"I love you. That's why I married you."

He grumbled under his breath as he walked away.

After he left, the nurse found me crying as I sat waiting for my mom to return to the hospital. "My husband is mad at me because I got pregnant," I told the nurse. "He's making me take a blood test."

"Honey, you know, it takes two people," she said and hugged my shoulder.

I cried. "He doesn't want a baby. He's claiming he's not the father."

"I'll talk to one of the doctors. Maybe he can have a talk with your JJ," she said comfortingly.

She came back shortly after. "While you're getting your blood drawn at the lab, the doctors are going to take your husband into the conference room and have a talk with him."

"Oh, no, there will be hell to pay. I don't think that's a good idea."

"Sure, it is. Trust me."

At noon, as they were drawing my blood, a doctor walked up to JJ. "Mr. Brown, can I talk to you for a moment?"

"Um, I have to make sure she finishes the test."

"I can assure you, she won't leave until the proper amount of blood is drawn. Just for a minute."

They entered the conference room where two other doctors were waiting.

"Mr. Brown, please have a seat," said the first doctor. "We understand you have some concerns about your wife's pregnancy?"

"I don't think I'm the father. We haven't been married that long, and I've been out of town most of the time."

"Did you have sex on your honeymoon?" one of the doctors asked.

"Well, sure," JJ bragged.

"Surely I need not tell you it only takes one time. Has your wife been unfaithful in the past?"

"Oh, no, she's very faithful," JJ boasted. "She won't even look at another man."

"Well, Mr. Brown, what's the problem?"

"She coerced me into marrying her. Besides, I'm too old to be a father. I don't have time to be a father. I'm a very busy man."

"Oh, really? How old is your wife?"

"She just turned thirty-five. So she'll be thirty-six when the child is born, and I'll be forty-five. That's too old to be parents. And what if it's a retard? That's not happening in my life!"

"Where do you live, Mr. Brown?"

"Portland, Oregon. I'm building her a dream log cabin over the border in Washington state."

"What about employment?" another of the doctors asked.

"Oh, yes. She's got a great job as a catering manager. I'm the architect for the Red Lions. In fact, I'm building a hotel right down the street from here."

"So you both make really good money. Sounds like a beautiful lifestyle for the three of you. I met your son. I worked on him in the emergency room."

"He's Bonnie's son, not mine. I just pay for him."

"Granted, your wife will be an older mother," the first doctor said, "but, Mr. Brown, you're sounding like a very ungrateful man. Many people would love to be in your position, even with a mongoloid child. You want to throw it all away because you think you're too old?" The doctor stood. "You should be ashamed of yourself. This baby is a gift. You need to be a man, suck it up and be grateful."

Another of the doctors said, "You need to go in there and apologize to your wife. You need to eat humble pie."

The first doctor said, "Regarding your concern about the child being mongoloid, there's a test your wife can take, a CVS sampling, a tissue from the fetus. It will determine not only if the child is yours but also if there are any abnormalities, like a missing chromosome, which is an indicator of Down Syndrome."

"The only way I will let her keep this baby," JJ said sternly, "is *if* you can prove to me this baby is *not* retarded or mongoloid. Otherwise, she is getting an abortion or a divorce!"

The nurse came back into Cody's room to enlighten me about the meeting between the doctors and JJ. "They had a little chat with your husband," she said, "and reassured him that he is quite capable of being a father and that he needs to own up to his responsibilities."

I jumped up with joy. "Really?"

"I'm amazed he hasn't come in and talked with you already. Has he been in to see you?"

"No. So, what's happens next?"

"Piece of cake. A CVS sampling tomorrow morning. It's a test that can tell you things like the sex of your child and how many chromosomes, stuff like that."

"I already know it's a girl."

"JJ is afraid that because you're older, the baby will be mongoloid."

"What?"

Cody woke then. "Mommy, what's wrong?"

"It's not that big of a deal, Bonnie," the nurse said. "You'll be in and out in no time."

JJ came in the next morning.

"Let me be perfectly clear," I said to him, poking him in the chest. "Even if I *don't* have enough chromosomes and it does turn out *she* has Down Syndrome, I will *not*, under any circumstance, have an abortion. You, my man, can count on that! I *will* raise this baby, with or without you. Just as I raised Cody, on my own!"

He grabbed my arm, hauled me out of the room and jerked me down the hall to the procedure room, dragging my feet all the way and all the while mumbling, "Just sign the damn papers! I don't have time for this!"

They knocked me out with anesthesia. She was not mongoloid. I knew that already. She was, after all, my destiny.

PART III
Molly's Childhood

CHAPTER FOURTEEN

Molly's Born!

JJ DIDN'T KNOW THE FIRST THING about loving someone—until the day Molly Mackenzie Brown was born, April 9, 1991, at Kaiser Permanente Hospital in Portland, Oregon.

The weeks prior to her birth, I made all the linens for her crib, the crib bumper, and the dust ruffles. JJ helped me paint her room and hang a wallpaper border. When I made the matching curtains, he appreciated my talent and insisted that I make curtains for our entire new house. He split the cost of the fabric with me.

I maintained a healthy diet, plus exercised. I didn't drink sodas or coffee. I wanted to give Molly the best chance possible at life. In the evenings, I treated her to classical music, laying a microphone on my belly each night as she and I slumbered into a restful sleep.

At birth, Molly was yellow with jaundice and eczema. Her liver wasn't functioning right. So she had to lie under ultraviolet lights, naked, to get the bilirubin in her white blood cells to adjust.

I hated that every other day, they'd cut the back of her tiny heel to squeeze out a drop of blood to check her blood count. I couldn't stand them doing that to my baby.

In July, JJ fell off a ladder and suffered a devastating concussion. He'd been putting a fireplace insert into our new chimney. He told his co-workers that I'd beat him up. I was not amused.

He refused to go to a doctor, and neither of us knew he had suffered a traumatic brain injury.

Almost immediately, his personality changed. It was subtle at first.

He changed his hairstyle and started combing it straight back. He stopped spending time with us on the weekends. I thought he was having an affair because he was never around. He stayed out later and later. I'd keep his dinner warm in the oven. He'd come in around eight p.m., just in time to read Molly a story, or to spank Cody for something that irritated JJ. Something was always irritating him.

But he developed a sweet relationship with Molly.

When she was two, one day the three of us were at the pool and he was teaching her how to hold her breath. He went under the water, held his breath, then finally popped up—and Molly, cute in a stripped bikini with goggles, said, "Daddy, what took you so long?"

Despite these tender moments, I knew JJ was mentally ill.

CHAPTER FIFTEEN

JJ Knocked Me Unconscious

I N 1993, JJ ASSAULTED ME. He knocked me unconscious. When I came to, I was incoherent and had a gash on the back of my head.

He'd been upset when I'd had a glass of wine without him. But I hadn't breastfed Molly for over a year, so I indulged myself. JJ had been traveling on business four nights a week.

I'd started crying, while holding Molly on my lap. "I didn't see you anymore. I miss our life together. You made me give up my all my friends!"

Cody had come out from his room, rubbing his eyes. "What's the matter, mommy?"

"It's okay, honey, just go back to bed. Daddy J and I are having a discussion." I tucked Cody back into bed.

JJ then began poking his finger into my shoulder. "I told you. You cannot have a glass of wine unless I am here to drink with you."

"But J, that's just so *unreasonable*. You can't make demands like that of me. Who do you think you are? You don't *own* me!"

"Oh, yes, I do! As long as you are living under *this* roof!" Memories of my father whirled in my mind.

Then JJ shoved me, hard, and I fell backwards, my head

slamming onto a corner of the wooden dining table, and I fell unconscious onto the carpet.

I woke to the flash of camera lights going off, JJ taking pictures of me passed out, then he shoved me with his foot.

"Oh, you're still alive," he quipped. He went into the bedroom and came out with his coat. "You're bleeding on the carpet," he said. "Make sure you clean that up before I get back!" And out the door he went, camera in hand. The beginning of many years of neglect, abuse, and unfaithfulness.

I'd been taught to call 911 if a crime occurred, and a crime had just occurred. So I did. You're not supposed to stick up for them, right?

Soon police were standing in my living room. "Do you want to make a report?" one of them asked.

I worried about that, while rubbing the goose egg on the back of my head, with my two young children standing behind me wondering what had happened.

I nodded.

They found him, in his office, and he had to spend the night in the slammer.

That night, JJ called his brother from jail. "The bitch called the cops on me. I need you to bail me out." And BIL drove the five hours from his house in Oregon.

The next morning, the doctor treating me was dumbfounded when I recounted the event. "He could have killed you," Dr. Kate said. "If you hadn't come out of the coma, he'd be looking at manslaughter charges."

After I got home with my babies, BIL confronted me at my house.

He sneered. "Why'd you call the cops on my brother! His job is in jeopardy now. You're stupid for getting the police involved. Come on. Get the kids. We have to go to the court house for his arraignment."

"Why do *we* have to go?"

"Because *you* are going to drop the domestic violence and assault charges against him."

The caseworker at the court house in Fort Vancouver Park, Washington urged me not to let JJ get away with this. "He did it once," she said, "and he'll try it again. The next time, he might just kill you."

I was so frightened that I didn't know what to do. I didn't want my children harmed. JJ wasn't the same man I had met in Colorado. Our lives had changed entirely after his fall off the ladder. Plus, with Cody's wolf attack, our lives had had a very rough start, I told myself.

While waiting for JJ's case to be heard, BIL sat beside me, and snarled. "You're disgusting. There's never been a Brown in a jail cell in the history of our family. Hasn't my brother done enough for you? You were *nothing* when he found you. You *will* drop these charges, or you will be sorry. I'll take your kids away from you, for drinking in front of them."

"Since when is that a *crime?*" I defended myself. "Why can't I have a glass of wine if the children are in bed?"

"You're an alcoholic! If it's the last thing I do, you'll drop all the charges—or I will make sure you're out on the street. I lent J $20,000 to build that house." He pointed his finger at me. "If you think *you're* going to get it, think again."

Threatened and coerced, I caved. I must keep my family together.

JJ was released with only anger-management classes. Outside the courtroom, he grabbed me firmly by the arm and ushered me to the car. "If you *ever* call the police on me again, I will kill you." He shoved me into the car. No apology.

I felt violated in so many ways.

JJ got out of attending anger-management, his attorney saying he was too busy. And the police let him walk, after a donation.

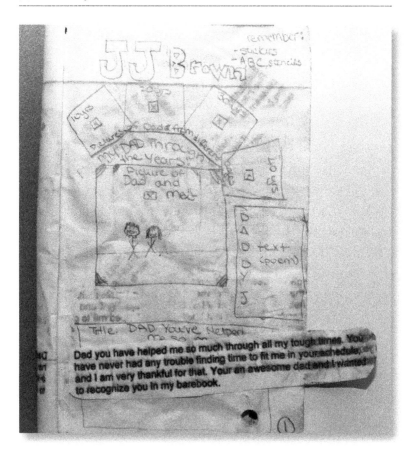

I was another statistic.

Dr. Kate wrote me a prescription for Prozac. I needed to numb the pain of my husband. But the pills made me emotionless. I didn't recognize who I was, and I lost all sense of myself. Most importantly, I lost my voice.

I survived only by going through the motions, happy on the outside. JJ made *me* attend marital counseling, but *he* never showed up. I felt so ashamed. I couldn't think of what I had done wrong.

Then two years later, 1995, he was fired from the Red Lions for sexual harassment and we had to move to Tennessee, the only place that would have him.

CHAPTER SIXTEEN

Discovering French Pastries
(Fat Shaming)

Now in Tennessee, when Molly was about seven, she and I decided to go to Daddy J's favorite fishing shop in downtown Memphis at the strip mall. We wanted to surprise him by buying a couple of new fishing flies for him. I let Molly pick out one on her own, knowing it was the best gift JJ would ever get.

Downstairs from the fly shop was my favorite French bakery, with the most scrumptious plump cakes, with all different contours of frostings that dripped with silver draggets perched on top.

That's where I found my love of Napoleon pastries. I teased myself, thinking, *I used to live in France,* because everything I loved in food was French. I delighted in raspberry-filled Napoleons, sandwiched between layers of custard-cream filling, a delicate layer of white frosting and a touch of chocolate between the lines. To die for! I didn't allow myself to have one very often.

This night at home, we placed JJ's special presents in front of his dinner plate.

But JJ also had a surprise: a bathroom scale, which he set on the kitchen floor.

"Cody, Molly, let's see if your mother's been a good girl this week."

I thought he was kidding, so I stepped on the scale and we watched the dial land on 135 pounds.

"Oh, no, children," JJ said somberly, "looks like Mother doesn't get any dinner tonight. She's too fat to have dinner with us. She only gets a glass of water. The other church ladies at Bellevue Baptist are much thinner than her."

He ceremoniously took away my filled dinner plate and dumped all the food into the kitchen sink. I grabbed at the plate but he pushed me away—and made me serve *them* a five-course meal with salad *and* dessert.

He had never before mentioned a specific weight. He had always seemed to be pleased with my appearance.

"What's wrong with my size?" I said. "I've always been this size."

"Exactly," he said.

But I did accept his judgment. Just as my mom had given in to my dad. Now I too was a victim of a bully. Why not? I had been bullied all my life.

I did not become anorexic, though. I had enough toxicity being bestowed on me.

However, immediately Molly did show signs of suffering from body dysmorphia. She started covering her mouth when chewing; and the next time JJ treated us to Baskin Robbins, she refused her favorite dessert. She would *not* have her daddy fat-shaming her, too.

CHAPTER SEVENTEEN

Opening Night

I N JANUARY 1998, when Molly was almost eight, she won a coveted set of tickets to the opening-night showing of the movie *Titanic*, starring Leonardo DiCaprio.

We had been listening to Celine Dione's theme song from the movie, and Molly had memorized it word for word and would slowly walk through the house, singing, "Near, far, wherever you are, we will go on."

JJ had just started proceedings for a legal separation. So now, I was sleeping in the back bedroom next to Molly's room.

Because of her big win, she wanted to go to the movie with Mommy, or Daddy. There were only two seats and she struggled to decide. She didn't want to hurt my feelings. But I knew she wanted a daughter-daddy date night. So I reassured her that we would watch it another time when it came out on VHS. And we did, many many times. She loved that movie! She pretended Leo was her boyfriend.

I found a darling blue-sapphire heart-shaped necklace for her to wear, her own "heart of the ocean" necklace as Kate Winslet had worn in the movie. Molly wore it with her velvet-satin dress that I bought for the special occasion, and she wore her white tights and black-satin Mary Janes to match.

I spent several hours preening Molly's hair into a top knot with cascading curls. We added a touch of color to her

lips and a smidgeon of mascara. She looked so grownup and sophisticated.

I waved goodbye to her as she and her father drove off in the Range Rover.

A radio station was at the opening. Big strobe lights lit up the sky, lights that Jennifer later would embrace on her own opening nights in L.A., Paris, and all over the world.

CHAPTER EIGHTEEN

Divorced

THE SUMMER OF 1998, JJ filed for divorce. The situation had also become unbearable for me. Actually three years earlier, after three months of living in Cordova. Throughout these years, JJ had alienated me from all my family and friends.

When Cody turned thirteen last year, JJ sent him to Patrick in Durango, Colorado, saying it was best for Cody during his teen years. After the many brutal spankings JJ had given Cody, I agreed it was the best choice.

Cody rarely popped into my life after he was sent away. Small wonder he changed his name when he turned eighteen. The last time I talked with him was in 2016. He was on his way by bus to his grandma's in Idaho but he never arrived. I am praying he is still alive.

Actually, for the last *twelve* years, JJ had systematically separated me from all I loved. I lost my identity, my family, and my friends.

So, now, I had finally started drinking.

"BB, if you don't stop drinking and find yourself a job, I'm going to divorce you."

"J, you make so much money I just want to stay home with the children," I begged him.

"I married a career woman. I made you into one. I will not tolerate a wife without a career!" he screamed at me, as the children looked on.

Immediately, I sobered up. I couldn't lose my family, my home, again. I started going to Bellevue Baptist Church's Wednesday-night rehab classes.

I did sign off on the divorce, reluctantly. Despite all his meanness and cruelty, despite the constant fighting, I loved JJ, with all my heart. I kept believing he would change his mind. I kept thinking he would come to his senses.

But he didn't.

Though JJ did file for divorce, we were still sleeping together. One night in bed, he said, "BB, you need to call off your lawyer. He's going to get most of our money if you keep him on. You must fire him. I insist. He's ripping you off. I'll give you half of everything we own. I promise. Fire him and we can both use my attorney, Wampler. He'll settle the divorce for half the price your attorney is charging you. You'll benefit more in the end."

I believed JJ.

That September, when I told the judge JJ and I were still having relations, he extended his decision to finalize our divorce.

JJ and I slept in different bedrooms for that entire year. I was on the other side of the house. It was painful having to sleep in the back bedroom, without him.

Nevertheless, I *still* slept with JJ, in *his* bed, his bedroom, on occasion. Well, it was sex only. On his part, not for love.

At the end of the judge's year-long extension, in September 1999, JJ said to me, "No, BB, you don't have to go to the hearing for our divorce. Wampler took care of everything and has set you up. You'll get half of everything."

Yet in the September 29th divorce decree, JJ got to keep almost everything in the house. I asked for a small cash settlement so Molly and I could begin our new lives.

JJ ended up with *all* of *our* art collection, as well as the Range Rover. I got to keep my 1988 Honda Civic that I'd had prior to the marriage. Though, with my proceeds from the divorce, I was finally able to buy a new 2000 Discovery Land Rover as a coming-out present for myself. I taught Molly to drive in that car, during our years in Grand Lake, and it is still waiting for her in storage when she returns.

The day the divorce was decreed, JJ gave me *one* month to move Molly and me to our own apartment. He kept the house.

October 1st, when Molly and I were moving our belongings, one of the moving guys told me, "Ma'am, did you know there's a *tap* on your phone? Did you know your husband is taping all of your phone calls?"

Then in November, the investment company holding my divorce payout told me the account was blocked and that I couldn't get the $100,000 until I turned sixty-two. If I took some of it now, I had to pay a fee of twenty percent, or $20,000. I needed that money to start over.

When I told JJ this, he just said, "Sounds like a personal problem to me."

That's when I knew I had been had.

PART IV
Molly' Style

CHAPTER NINETEEN

Molly's First Professional Paid Performance

M OLLY HAD ALWAYS IMITATED the people in her life. She had learned to play many roles.

In September 2000, after the divorce, when she was nine, I enrolled her in ballet classes. Memphis afforded many types of arts and culture, good amidst all the bad.

I encouraged Molly to experience everything her chubby little body could do. She hadn't yet reached puberty and her little cheeks were rounder than most. Though to me, that was one of her cutest features.

After a few months of lessons, Molly was chosen to be in the Memphis Ballet troupe's 2000 Christmas performance at the famous Orpheum Theatre. It was her *first* professionally paid appearance. Her *next* ballerina performance was in the movie *Red Sparrow* when she played a Russian spy.

Before Molly was given the part in the Memphis troupe, we hadn't heard anything about parts being awarded to the younger children, especially not paid parts. We'd only heard rumors as we listened to the prima donna older girls, with their long sleek legs, talking in the dressing room. All of them had hopes of being the lead ballerina as Clara for that year's performance in the *Nutcracker*.

One fall afternoon, I was watching Molly and the other ballerinas her age practicing their plies in their pink leotards, hair pinned up in buns, when a tall unfamiliar woman approached the girls. She wore a leotard covered with a wrap skirt, her hair tightly knotted in a bun on top of her head. *A grownup version of my little girl*, I thought.

During Molly's six-month check-up as an infant, her pediatrician had told me Molly would be tall, as much as six feet. And Molly often asked me, while growing up, "So, when is this growth spurt going to happen?"

"Soon enough, Molly girl."

The tall ballet mistress encouraged the boys and girls who were practicing to the rhythmic metronome. "That's right. 1-2-3, 1-2-3."

Then they formed into a large circle around the perimeter of the wall alongside the bars. With their arms held high, they stretched up their fingertips as far as they could reach. Then round and round they went, rhythmically in a large circle, poised gracefully, heads high, imitating butterflies leaving their cocoons, becoming what they were meant to be: the most beautiful of butterflies.

I watched in awe. It was the first time I'd seen Molly emanate such grace.

The ballet mistress went around and touched the heads of seven girls and two boys, including Molly. They then settled onto the floor quietly, crossed their legs, and folded their hands in their laps.

The other children were dismissed and they scurried out of the room politely.

Then the ballet mistress waved over us moms and dads. We slipped off our shoes and joined her on the polished wooden floor.

"Your child has been chosen to take part in the *Nutcracker* performances December 15 through 17 for the holidays." She

spoke with a heavy Russian accent. "I am with the International World Ballet Troupe. We have a lot of work to do and your child's practice time will be doubled now. If you are unable to make this time commitment, speak now so we can find a suitable replacement." All of us parents looked at each other in awe. Our children all cheered at once, stood up and ran to us.

Molly grabbed onto me, hugging me with all her might. "Can I, Mommy?" she pleaded, red-faced with excitement. "Can I, please, please?"

"Absolutely," I assured her as I picked her up and swung her into my arms. "Won't your daddy be pleased?"

She was chosen for all three performances Friday, Saturday matinee, and Sunday. Some of the children didn't get to perform opening night, but Molly did.

"You are a chosen one, my Molly girl," I told her. "Molly Brown is your name, and you are my unsinkable daughter."

She clapped her hands in delight as I held her tight all the way out the door to our awaiting green Land Rover.

CHAPTER TWENTY

Making History

I N THE COUNTRY MILES from downtown Memphis, in the
middle of nowhere, in Braden known for its famous hole-
in-the-wall chicken restaurant *Gus's Chicken*, I named my
antique store *Molly n' Me*.

I bought the turn-of-the-century building with the proceeds from the divorce. Little did I know I was creating history, because buying the building required having a law added
to the record books. In Tennessee, women had not before
been allowed to own property, at least not without a man's
signature on the deed. Only men had been allowed to sign for
a note. They passed a law for me.

The five-acre property, dating back to the early 1800s,
owned by the McGraw family for over a hundred years, had
included the only general store east of the Mississippi. This
fantastic three-story brick building had a hand-pull elevator
for a cotton gin that had operated on the top floor.

The back of the property had housed a makeshift hospital
for soldiers during the Civil War. I often saw people with
metal detectors rummaging over grave sites, looking for but-
tons from the officers who had been buried beneath the
earth. Remnants of wagon-wheel ruts still crossed the south
forty.

This land also had housed a bank and post office. One of my favorite treasures inherited with the building was a black bank safe, with a Wells Fargo painting on the front.

I filled the 20,000-sq. foot building to the brim with thrift-store and auction finds. Downtown Memphis was a treasure trove of memorabilia. Now and then, my new friend Bessie, an old black woman, came into the store and warmed herself at my wood stove, which I kept going full time during the winter. I couldn't afford to heat the store otherwise, plus the fire was a perfect nostalgic addition as it illuminated my antiques. On occasion, Bessie whipped up homemade biscuits and we'd sit by the fire, in antique rocking chairs, and eat them as she told stories about the McGraw property's illustrious past.

When I later sold the store in 2002, to move back to Colorado to open my Grand Lake store, the new owners turned the building into a catfish restaurant. That's when they discovered in the basement, next to the elevator, a den of the world's largest concentration of copperhead snakes ever found, right *below* the fireplace that had opened onto my makeshift bedroom for Molly and me.

That explained why another friend, Mac, had insisted I not live there. He too had found a snake, curled up on a door knob, coiled around it. Thinking it was one of Molly's jump ropes, he had grabbed at it.

Oops!

Lucky Molly and me. Unscathed during our delightful years there.

CHAPTER TWENTY-ONE

Full Custody

THE SUMMER OF 2001 when Molly and I were still in Braden, JJ and I had been divorced two years and I was awarded full custody of her.

As he traveled a great deal all over the world, designing hotels, Molly had lived with me ninety percent of the time, vacationing with him the other ten percent. My having full custody fit JJ's schedule better.

Then that summer, he enrolled Molly at a satellite **Camp Hi Ho,** a horseback-riding academy at the camp in Bartlett, twenty miles west of my antique store, for two weeks during the Tennessee summers.

One afternoon, he called me to let me know he was running late and asked me to pick up Molly at the camp.

He was busy finding her a cowboy hat for her evening equestrian performance to show off her barrel-racing skills. She was graduating that night. Molly was always a natural with horses. She had learned to ride in Grand Lake, Colorado during our summer vacations.

I wiped the sparkle from my brow as I jumped into my Land Rover to go pick up Molly at the stables. Southern ladies only sparkled. They never sweat.

That afternoon at the equestrian camp, while I watched Molly galloping along the fence line, riding her favorite horse, *Oreo,* dark stormy clouds formed out of nowhere.

The horse trainer, **Karen Lawrence**, called out to Molly, "The lightening's getting pretty close. You'd better get inside."

Then the sky broke loose in a violent storm.

We hurried inside a rough n' tumble trailer. As I entered, shaking off the rain, I reached out to shake Karen's hand. "Hi. I'm Bonnie Brown, Molly's mom."

She refused it. "I know."

She plopped us down at a makeshift kitchen table, then tossed towels into a clothes dryer. Cowboy music billowed in the background. Molly and I stared at one another.

I carried on and on, spewing whatever was on my mind, despite my dad's warning, *Children are to be seen and not heard.*

"My husband just divorced me," I rambled. "We were together fifteen years. We were the perfect all-American family. We moved to this God-forsaken place six years ago, from God's country, Vancouver, Washington. My husband designed and built a beautiful log home as my wedding gift, a cabin mansion fit for a queen. I even got to pick out the color of the sink, fire-engine red to match all the knobs in the kitchen. My husband is a famous architect, plus he has a degree in art, two degrees actually." I spoke proudly.

No finished degrees for me, I thought to myself. I was the weak link. It had been only a matter of time until JJ realized his mistake in marrying me. I had known I wasn't worthy of his love.

I went on bragging about how handsome JJ was. "He's the smartest man I ever met, smarter than President Ford. I worked for him, you know. I was his personal chef. I lived with them in their homes at Rancho Mirage and Beaver Creek, Colorado. I traveled with them. I even made cookies for the Secret Service." I tried to make myself look important and significant. I really hadn't been anything more than an indentured slave.

And JJ had only married me because I was a good cook. He only wanted someone to bed every night, and that's what he liked best. I believe he had a sex addiction.

Plus, he wanted me to look after him, like his mom had.

TWENTY-TWO

The Simple Life

SEPTEMBER 2001, I put my antique shop in Braden up for sale and stored our belongings in the building until I could move them to Grand Lake.

"Molly, honey, we're going to move to Colorado and live in Grandma's cabin. Your daddy has chosen not to be a part of my life anymore. We will be pioneer women, like you studied in school last year. It's a little secluded mountain town, with clean air."

I felt our souls needed rejuvenation, free of the large city. It's where I had always gone to decompress. It was my safety net, my safe harbor.

We moved right after 9/11, back to the cabin, where Molly had been conceived. She was ten.

I rented a 5x8 U-Haul, added trailer lights and brakes to the Land Rover and off we went.

We spent my forty-sixth birthday in our new home, and Molly attended fifth grade at Grand Lake Elementary, less than a mile away.

"Your cousins went to that school. I just know you will thrive here."

She was a trooper.

Getting Molly ready for school in the mornings was always an adventure. We'd always had water problems at Mom's cabin. The pump would groan as it reached its limit. The copper pipe in the basement would *clang clang clang*, rattling the upstairs hardwood floor, warning, *I'm almost out of water.*

I'd wake up at six a.m. and grab my first cup of percolated coffee. While waiting for water to boil for oatmeal, I'd place chipped kindling and crumpled newspaper under the grate in the fireplace, then add small logs in the shape of a teepee, so the cabin would be warm before Molly got up.

At night, I'd flip a coin. "Heads or tails, Molly?"

"Tails, Mommy."

That meant we'd turn on the electric blanket. The cabin had no heat. If the coin landed on heads, we turned on the space heater next to our bed. With only 40 amps of electricity in the cabin, the breakers constantly flipped all night. The cabin was meant for summer only, when we only needed a pile of blankets to keep us warm. My grandfather had stuffed the cracks and crevices in the walls with minimal insulation.

During particularly frigid nights, we could see our breath in the air. But Molly and I just snuggled closer.

Before I could turn the heater on in the bathroom, the oatmeal had to be finished and the stove turned off in the kitchen.

"Molly girl. It's time to wake up, sleepy head."

She'd open her eyes, glad to be awake, and ready herself for whatever adventures awaited her for the day. She'd reach up and wrap her arms around my neck. "I love you, Mommy."

"I love you, too, Molly." Then I'd gently coax her out of her warm bed.

We only washed our hair on the weekends. Because her hair was long and took extra time to dry, I thought an extra wink of sleep was more important.

In the shower, the water was on just long enough to get soaped up. Then we turned it off, before the pipes groaned. Then on again to rinse and finish washing our faces. We had to be quick—so we wouldn't run out of water.

We dried off in front of the space heater, then ran into the living room to the awaiting fire, which was roaring by that time. Molly's clothes were all laid out on Grandma's ottoman and were warm and toasty for her to slip into. She'd pick her outfit the night before, so I could have it ready.

After-School Cooking Lessons

I secured a position thirty miles away in Hot Sulphur with the Grand County Historical Museum, working until 2:30 p.m. Mondays through Thursdays since Molly got out of school at 3:00.

Fewer than a hundred students attended Molly's school. There were mostly ten students to one teacher, and Molly quickly made friends her own age.

With the museum sponsoring, I put together an after-school program at the Granby Charter School for seventh and eighth graders, and taught cooking lessons to the kids, ensuring that they would have an after-school snack.

Molly was my assistant, and she took her job very seriously. On the weekends, she helped me to prepare the lesson plan, and we went to City Market to purchase the ingredients for our recipe. As we walked the aisles with our list, she would read from the index card while I plucked the ingredients off the shelves. When each item was added to our grocery cart, she added it mentally, pencil on paper, and we stuck to our budget.

One of Molly's favorite recipes in the students' cooking class was popcorn balls. We would all butter our hands, then shape the popcorn mixture into baseball sizes. Then Molly would instruct the students, "Carefully tear off a piece of your favorite-colored saran wrap. Only one piece now."

She liked overseeing the older kids. Plus, after we were done cooking, we got to take home the remaining treats.

Molly's Slumber Party

As Molly got older, I wanted all her friends to like me, just as my girlfriends in Newport Beach had liked my Grandma after our beach-house party.

Our second year at the cabin, when Molly returned from summer vacation with her dad, I wanted to show her an equally enjoyable time.

The week before school was to start, I rented two cabins at The Grand Lake Lodge, near where we lived, and I took Molly and her six girlfriends horseback riding at Winding River, so Molly could show off her equestrian skills. Most of the girls had never ridden a horse, but we had a great camp guide.

Molly and her girlfriends also got to swim in the pool and go in the Jacuzzi. Plus, I also let them order takeout from the restaurant, with an open tab. (Molly made sure all their requests were thoughtfully garnered. No one overindulged or wore out their welcome.)

Later, we all settled at the bright campfire and made s'-mores, roasting marshmallows on long sticks over the blazing fire, then squeezed with Hershey milk chocolate bars between graham crackers. Yum!

After our delightful treat, we went back to the slumber-party cabin and the girls all told stories. Molly read from a book she'd brought from Tennessee, *Harry Potter,* and they all became Hogwart crazed.

Molly inspired her friends with her storytelling just as she inspires us today with her films.

CHAPTER TWENTY-THREE

Teenage Angst

A<small>T AGE THIRTEEN,</small> Molly was edgy, always snapping and disrespectful. She criticized me every chance she got, belittling and degrading me, telling me I wasn't good enough. Oddly, the very same words JJ had said to me during the divorce.

Christmas 2004, right before it was time to take Molly to the airport to go visit him, she snarled at me. "Dad's asking his girlfriend to marry him. And I am moving to Tennessee and going to high school *there*. I am going to live with *them*. *You* will be broke." Then she flippantly ran out the door.

I was being replaced. I didn't even know he was dating, let alone getting married. A dagger through my heart.

Did Molly's impudence make it easier for her to leave me behind? Last summer, her Girl Scout leader had told me she was the *only* girl who had made her Build a Bear for her mommy. I do know that JJ convinced Molly I was not good enough for her.

So, she'd made up her mind that nothing would keep her away from her dad, no matter what.

I tried not to overreact. Though I did ask, who was the woman, when did they start dating, was she prettier than me.

Molly just shrugged it off. "Daddy said not to tell you *anything*."

And she didn't. I didn't learn a thing about his new woman.

I was a wreck the entire Christmas. Some bimbo was stealing my family away from me. I had expected JJ to rekindle our relationship. Instead, he had moved on.

Then when Molly returned and was coming down the ramp from the plane, she was visibly upset.

Things had *not* gone her way on the trip—and she was going to make *my* life miserable.

It didn't take much to tick her off. Like her father, she was a very high-strung Aries, also high-maintenance. Life had to be perfect or there was hell to pay.

Then I learned that Molly was upset because JJ's proposal had been refused—because he was still "in love" with *me*, Molly explained. She would no longer work as a busser for Lin at the Chinese restaurant nor with her friend at The Sagebrush

So, it was *my* fault. Molly had envisioned no longer having a care in the world, a grand life with her dad, and a *new* mom.

CHAPTER TWENTY-FOUR

Run, Girl, Run!

THE NEXT APRIL, 2005, Molly returned from Spring Break in Tennessee with her daddy after she had just turned fourteen. We'd planned to celebrate ourselves when she came home, a trip to Breckenridge or Steamboat Springs.

She returned with a new sport. Running.

JJ had run the entire time I knew him, and he had made it quite clear that's how I should keep myself in shape as well.

So I had. I had jogged around the entire back bay of Jantzen Beach, Oregon, three miles, wearing headphones over my Princess Leia buns. Before I knew it, I looked forward to jogging. It made me feel healthy.

Now Molly had a spring in her step. When JJ had left her alone in Tennessee to go running himself, she had tagged along.

I was proud of her will power, although concerned with her jogging through the meadow in the early morning hours. Bears were emerging from their winters naps, and mountain lions were protecting their cubs.

So, I went along in the cold morning air, with the snow barely off the ground. She left me far behind.

So then I followed in the Land Rover, keeping my distance, just to look out for her. This was *her* thing.

Then Molly joined the track team, and ran her heart out. I went to all of her track meets, in and out of town. Some were a hundred miles away. As often as I could, I chaperoned, taking homemade cupcakes plus Kool-Aid for the team.

The end-of-season track meet in early May was in Kremmling, Colorado. It was only forty-five mountain miles, but an hour-and-a-half by Land Rover.

That Saturday, I left a sign on the door of our boutique gift shop, The Flannel Antler, that I wouldn't be open until afternoon.

On that frigid day, I felt so sorry for the girls having to take off their jackets and sweat pants, wearing only skimpy shorts and sleeveless tops. It was 45 degrees outside and Molly had just returned from 70-degree weather in Memphis.

Though our team was missing a few girls, a skeleton crew, this was the final meet of the season and they all gave it their best.

One by one, the girls ran the events: first the 25-meter, next the 50. Then Molly had an event, and she placed second in a sprint. She was devastated at her loss. She loved being first, and thrived in competitions. She wanted to win ribbons!

I walked alongside her as she cooled down, brushing the hair from her face. "You did good, Molly."

On the verge of tears, she barely acknowledged me.

The coach yelled, "Shake it out, Molly!"

We circled back and she gulped from the water cooler.

They announced third place. Second place, Molly Brown. First place. Underneath all the clapping, Molly flipped off the win as if to say, *Yeah, right. Second place. Yeah yeah yeah.* She just wanted to get on with the next event.

As the meet continued, it was announced that in order for our team to qualify for recognition awards or participation ribbons, we had to be represented in the final run. The 1200 meter was three times around the track. Then our coach walked over to our team and said we were leaving, that the meet was over.

"Coach, what do you mean?" Molly asked, stunned.

"We don't have a runner for the 1200. We thought she was showing up, but she hasn't."

One of the girls starting crying. Another asked, "So we don't get *our* ribbons?"

"I'm sorry, girls. Better luck next year," he said.

"What about me, coach?" Molly piped up. "What about *me*, coach?" she said again, pacing. "The team should get the honors they deserve."

"Molly, no," he said, "you've never run that distance."

Everyone looked at her. They knew Molly didn't have the endurance training needed, and she had just gotten back from Memphis, which was a different oxygen level.

"No!" she said. "I'm *in*! Go sign me up. The team *will* get their ribbons. We'll place in the meet. *I'll do it!*"

I hugged her. "You don't have to do this, honey. It'll be okay."

She looked at me. "No, Mom. You don't understand. I have to. For the *team*."

I hugged her tight and whispered, "I know, Molly Girl. I know. I'll be right here with you." We both then said a prayer for strength and endurance.

The race was on! People stood, and applause rang throughout the crowd.

Molly peeled off her sweat pants and hoodie, then flapped her arms, getting ready.

"Love you," I said.

"Love you, too, Mom."

She placed her foot in the crouch position. The starter pistol fired. She ran fast.

Running. Just running. Focused. Her ponytail bouncing.

As she completed the first lap around the track, she slowed a bit.

"You got it, Molly Girl!" I shouted.

All the other runners had already started their last lap. All of Molly's team mates shouted her name from the distance.

"You can do it, Molly!"

Her face flushed noticeably red.

After her second lap, she stopped and chugged a big gulp of water. I saw the desperation in her face.

"You've got this!" I shouted.

Focused, she took off again.

"You're almost there!" I shouted.

Her lungs were burning. She had asthma for Heaven's sake! She was recovering from mono. I should have told her no. Tears streamed down my face, wanting the best for her.

She was walking now, holding her side, but still on course.

The coach ran up beside her. "Molly, you can stop now. It's okay."

She looked at him. "NO. IT'S NOT OKAY! I am NOT done!"

Runner's euphoria kicked in just then and she picked up speed.

She rounded the final hundred meters, and her entire team started running next to her. I was running. The coach was running. The crowd was cheering! All the way to the finish line—right through the yellow ribbon across the track, her arms raised high in victory.

"I did it!" she yelled. "I finished!"

The coach lifted her up and held her high for all the crowd to see. My beautiful girl.

They all got ribbons that day, and Molly got a special recognition in everyone's hearts.

CHAPTER TWENTY-FIVE

It Took Brain Surgery

IN EARLY JUNE 2005, at eight in the morning, I was driving Molly to East Grand Middle School where she was in the eighth grade. It was a nice day, the sun was out.

Molly was sniffling.

"Is everything okay?"

She looked away from me, out her window.

We approached the red farm house where we would turn up the hill, the halfway mark from school. Again I asked and she finally turned to me, tears streaming, fists clenched, and sobbing. "Daddy is in the hospital! He's having brain surgery. This morning."

I hit the brakes. "Brain surgery?"

She had been on the phone with him last night. I thought they were just making plans for her upcoming summer visit.

"It's the size of a grapefruit! . . . Mom, I want to go help him recuperate."

I pulled over to the side of the road, pierced with shock.

I shut off the car, patted her cheek with my hankie and took her in my arms. "Surely you are mixed up about why Daddy J is in the hospital?"

She sobbed hysterically, barely catching her breath. "No, Mom. You don't understand. Daddy said *goodbye* to me last night—in case he doesn't make it out of surgery. He said, no matter what, he will be with me forever in Heaven. That I just need to think about him when I look up at the stars." She turned to me. "He told me to be strong for him. That he doesn't want to leave me, but if it is God's will, let his will be done."

I was crying, too. Surely God wouldn't be that cruel. Both Molly and I needed him. We both loved him. I never thought I would lose JJ forever.

I needed to be strong for Molly, and for him. I turned the car around and we drove back home, praying all the way.

The next day when JJ woke up in the hospital, he phoned me. He was barely out of the anesthesia. I'll never forget that conversation.

"BB, why aren't we married anymore?"

I thought I was hallucinating.

"While I was under, God spoke to me. I made him a promise. If he'd let me live, I would be a more loving husband to you. I saw into our future. We will be together, as a happy family, for eternity."

Thank you, Jesus! My prayers had been answered.

It was as if the last ten years hadn't happened. JJ was back. The man I had fallen in love with, in the kitchen, washing dishes and talking about going fishing together. The man he was *before* he fell off the ladder, fourteen years ago.

JJ and I began making plans to remarry, in July. Molly went back to Tennessee to take care of him and to solidify our plans for getting remarried. Or so I thought.

I put my gift shop The Flannel Antler on the market, as well as my Grand Lake house and condo. I stored all my personal belongings in Mom's cabin. It was always my home. Mom and I had an understanding. I was the only one of my

siblings who had put any effort into the cabin to fix it up. I loved the cabin.

I was eager to return to Tennessee to marry JJ. It had been a very long time since he'd wrapped his arms around me in love.

I didn't realize, then, that Molly hated that JJ and I were getting remarried. She had told all her best friends—Kayla Schrader, Lindsey and countless others—she was *not* returning to Grand Lake in the fall. She was entering ninth grade in Memphis, for the horseback riding, abundance of boys, and shopping malls.

She had gone back to talk her daddy out of marrying me. She hadn't planned on him waking up from the surgery and still being in love with me.

The idea of our re-marriage had put a kink in her fourteen-year-old plans. She no longer would be the center of his attention, and she would *not* share him with anyone.

CHAPTER TWENTY-SIX

The Greatest Shock

FOR MONTHS, MOLLY HAD BEEN telling me this fantasy of hers, of going to high school in Tennessee and living with her daddy.

Each time she had brought it up, I said, "Over my dead body." Not after JJ had forced Cody into leaving home. I certainly wouldn't let him take away my daughter, too. A girl needs her mother.

Then without telling me, JJ had gone to the high school in Cordova—with the hospital bandage from the brain surgery around his head—and they had allowed him to enroll Molly, at her persuasion: "Mom is coming here soon, and school is starting."

August 2005, just after the three o'clock bell, Molly was sitting outside patiently, completing her homework, waiting for her father to pick her up—for three hours.

She watched the last teacher leave the parking lot. It was growing dimmer and dimmer outside. Weird boys were driving by and checking her out, staring as she sat alone.

Still, she sat there, time ticking by slowly. Tick tick tick. Dad was always on time. Where was he?

She sat there perplexed, not knowing what to do. The car full of unruly boys circled a few more times and blatantly stared longer and harder.

When they drove away this time, Molly ran and hid behind a column at the school front, sobbing and wiping away tears. "Daddy J, where are you?"

Finally, she began to find her way home. It was survival time.

She knew better than to walk alongside the road. Those boys would come looking for her.

In the dark, under a full moon, she cut through the fields, along the creek, through the vineyard, past the railroad tracks, and through the weeds, with the summer thistle prickling her face, five miles to JJ's house—in Memphis, a city with one of the highest murder rates.

But Molly wouldn't let herself be afraid.

It took her over an hour to finally find the street, East Wood Mills Cove.

In the black night, the moon now shadowed by clouds, she peered through the garage door window. His car was there.

She hurried anxiously to the front door and, trembling, searched under the urn for the key, knowing something was terribly wrong.

She slammed the door open onto the rack of plants inside, sending them clamoring to the tile floor, glass and pottery breaking, and ran through the entry hall and living room.

"Daddy! Where are you?"

The dining room and the kitchen.

"Daddy!"

The bedroom.

He was lying on the bed.

Napping, she first thought and smirked. "Daddy, you forgot to pick me up."

She approached the bed. He wasn't moving. His arms were over his chest, his hands clasped, as if praying.

She shook him madly. "Wake Up. WAKE UP!"

His hands fell to his sides.

She put her ear to his chest. "You're still breathing!"

She gathered him up, sliding her arm under his back, and pulled upward with great force, cuddling him, shaking him. "Wake up! Open your eyes!"

She tried to pry an eye open. He slid out of her arms, too heavy. He slumped over and fell to the floor.

She ran to the kitchen landline phone and called Cathy, screaming, "Daddy J didn't pick me up from school! I found him lying on his bed! He's still breathing!"

"Oh, my God, Molly. Hang up and call 911."

Shortly after, paramedics wrapped JJ in a blanket, put him on a gurney, and slid him into the ambulance. They had to pry Molly off him, her fists clenched around his forearm.

"It's going to be alright, Daddy!" she cried to him.

As the ambulance pulled away, she prayed. "You are still alive, Daddy. You'll rally. You always come back to me."

My All-Time Low

K NOWING NONE OF THIS, and believing that Molly was helping JJ prepare our wedding while I sold The Flannel Antler, I called JJ's house to say hello to my soon-to-be betrothed, excited to hear his voice again.

BIL answered. BIL?

Confused, I asked, "Where's J?"

BIL took a deep breath. "He died, Bonnie."

Sorrow plunged through me. "Died? What do you mean?" I began to sob hysterically and could hardly catch my breath. "What happened? Is Molly okay? Where is she?"

"Molly found him. He's been in the hospital, in a coma. . . I was at his bedside. He came out of the coma and didn't know where he was. He pulled out his IV, to go to the bathroom. When he stood, he fell and his head hit the floor."

The words began to sink in. Gone?

I walked aimlessly around the store, cell phone to my ear. "We were getting remarried," I mumbled.

"Bonnie, I sat with him as he took his last breath. He was gasping. It was awful. His jaw became rigid. I had to close his mouth."

"Why are you telling me this!" I couldn't bear to hear this. Heartbroken, I whispered, "Where's Molly?"

"At a friend's house."

"I can't believe she didn't call me."

"She's pretty traumatized."

"When's his funeral?"

"We cremated him, a few days ago."

I felt faint. "And you didn't call me . . . ?"

"The services are tomorrow."

"Tomorrow?"

"Tomorrow morning."

Faint, I whispered, "I can't get there in time. . . I want to talk to Molly."

"She's safe, Bonnie. . . . Too bad you won't be able to attend."

I felt gut-punched, in more ways than one.

Molly called me the next afternoon. I ached to hold her. I gathered myself. "Molly, I'm glad you had time with your daddy. I'll come get you."

"I'm in school here now. Daddy signed me up. I want to stay."

She had told me, and I hadn't wanted to hear it. She had wanted to live with her daddy.

Devastated myself by his loss, and wanting Molly to be happy, I acquiesced.

CHAPTER TWENTY-EIGHT

The Lost Opportunities

B IL WAS TRYING TO TAKE Molly away from me. He tried. Oh, how he tried.

The day I had put JJ in jail for the spousal abuse, BIL had vowed to me that he would vindicate his brother. Was it that? Or more, the appeal of the million-dollar estate left to Molly?

My lawyer said the court case would take many months and advised me to set up residency in Tennessee, to strengthen my case for retaining custody and to show that my commitment to Molly was unbounded by where I lived, that I would go anywhere for her.

I already had sold The Flannel Antler, my house and condo. So I was here to stay, for as long as it took to get back Molly's heart.

I rented a two-bedroom apartment in Cordova, where she was attending ninth grade.

Yet Molly didn't want to stay with *me*. She was staying with JJ's friend, Cathy, and she had been telling all her friends she was an orphan.

Being back in Memphis was surreal with JJ gone and all my dreams gone with him.

Molly barely spoke to me. Our once tight-bond had unraveled. Somehow. And I didn't know why.

I wanted to make it up to her. I wanted to smother her with love.

Shopping had always cheered up Molly, so I asked to meet her after school to go to the new Galleria Carriage Crossing. But she cancelled at the last minute, saying she had other plans.

So I went by myself. I would take her another time.

Macy's was full of designer shoes, accessories, and clothes. I found myself a pair of Cole Hahn's mule-slide boots. It had been a long time since I had purchased something new and nice.

As the clerk was wrapping the boots, I saw five teenage girls making a fuss in the evening-gowns section. *What fun!* I thought.

They looked about Molly's age, all scurrying about, grabbing elaborate bejeweled ball gowns and carrying them into the dressing rooms.

Then I thought I saw Molly darting into a dressing room. *Let it be her!* I hoped. Did she see me?

Then one of the girls called out her name. "Molly, look at this one."

"Molly?" I went up to the door. "Molly, is that you?"

She opened the door, ball gown half on. "Mom, what you are you doing here?" She pulled me inside, while all of her girlfriends gathered around outside the door.

"Well, I decided to go shopping. . . You couldn't come. . . I just wanted to check it out."

"You'll ruin everything!"

My heart sank. I was just missing her. I hid my disappointment and pretended to be cheerful. "So, why are you trying on these fancy dresses?"

She sighed. "I'm looking for a homecoming dress for the Prom. I've been nominated for the Freshman Homecoming Princess."

Of course you have! My heart warmed with love for my little girl, still fourteen.

"Oh, I can get it for you," I said brightly.

"I have a credit card."

"A credit card?" I blurted out.

Proudly, she confided. "Uncle BIL gave it to me."

"What's the credit limit?"

"Five thousand."

"Five-thousand dollars?" I said in shock. "I'll have to talk to him about that."

Why would he give her such access? I wondered. That felt so off. Something didn't feel right.

Seeing the shock on my face, and undoubtedly my hurt, Molly said, "Just go back to Colorado. You're ruining everything."

I slinked out of the dressing room, past her friends, hearing them say, "Who was that?"

"My mom," she said, shrugging and rolling her eyes.

"I thought you didn't have a mom?" they said in chorus, eyebrows puzzled.

"It's a long story."

My all-time low. A Molly I had never seen before.

I slunked my way to my rental car, dragging the fancy bag with my insignificant boots.

Each visit with Molly was more strained: through Thanksgiving, through Christmas, through the New Year, even though these were our first holidays without JJ.

The more I tried to do for Molly, the more she pulled away. Our visits felt like it was only an obligation for her. She responded in one-word sentences. She acted like she resented me. I had lost her. What had I done wrong?

I needed to reach Molly, somehow. I would work doubly hard.

For Valentine's Day 2006, I wanted Molly to feel the same love I had for her.

At the jewelry counter at Macys, on my cell phone I talked to Molly's best friend Kayla Schrader, trying to choose the perfect gift for my sweet valentine. It had to be just right, especially this year.

"Kayla, which do you think? The ring with a garnet heart and two diamonds set in gold? The heart-shaped earrings? Or the necklace with a solid red heart?"

"Umm, Mom," Kayla said, "I think the ring and the necklace. Molly doesn't wear many earrings."

"Thanks, Kayla! You're right."

But I bought all three. Molly needed splurging on. I had learned that from JJ. When he wanted to make up, he'd come home with jewelry.

Molly already had Valentine's plans that evening with Cathy and her fourteen-year-old daughter. But she did agree to meet me for lunch at a café.

I was excited as she opened each of the three boxes and accepted my gifts, politely. She wasn't full of gleeful joy, as in our past.

I clasped the necklace around her neck. She touched it nervously.

We then called Kayla.

"Is it beautiful?" Kayla asked Molly. ". . . You're so lucky to have your mom."

"Yeah, lucky," Molly mumbled, and quickly hung up.

The next day, I asked Molly what Cathy thought of the gifts.

"I couldn't wear them in front of her," she said. "That would be bragging. I didn't want to make her feel bad. But I showed them to her, and she said she liked them."

I liked that Molly was sensitive to her friend's feelings, but it hurt that she didn't wear them after that. She never got the ring sized, and she wore the earrings only one time. She wasn't the Molly girl I had raised.

I later heard that Molly had told a story at church that I was drunk every time I took her out.

The thing is, I was *never* intoxicated. Sometimes I'd had one, maybe two, glasses of wine with our meal. It was Cathy getting leverage to get custody of Molly, with BIL's help.

BIL was helping Cathy to *adopt* Molly, and Cathy did everything she could to trip me up. Once, when I picked up Molly at school for a day of fun, I hoped, Cathy raked me over the coals, "You are an unfit mother!"

The Valentine's gifts were a reminder to Molly, I am your real momma.

I had always had full custody of Molly.

No one told me that as Molly's sole custodial parent, I could have moved into JJ's house in Tennessee and resumed custody without any problem. BIL knew and he didn't tell me.

He also made me pay him, the estate executor, to buy back my memories and my own things, that I knew Molly would want in the future.

Almost on TV

Then came Molly's first birthday without her daddy, April 2006.

One day after I picked her up from Cordova High School, Cathy called me and said a local television studio needed my permission for a short they were filming that afternoon with Molly. Apparently, Molly was quite the wiz with cell-phone texting and had beat out her classmates as the fastest message-sender *during* class. She had even bragged about how she was able to hide it from the teachers, as she wasn't *supposed* to be texting during class.

But she had been captured on video, and the TV announcer was going to expose Molly, showing her disrespecting her teachers. I wasn't excited.

However, Molly pleaded with me. It was her big opportunity to be on TV. So I met with the producer that afternoon. By then, however, they already had used an alternate for the part.

Molly was crushed and wept uncontrollably. Red-faced, she yelled at me, "I hate you, Mom! You've ruined my life! I will *never* forgive you! I wanted to be on TV!"

The producer put his arm around her shoulder and tried to explain that it wasn't my fault, and that he would make sure she had another opportunity to be on the news, that she was a natural. "A different time," he promised.

She shoved him aside. "No, you won't. You didn't use me this time. I'll never see you again." And off she stormed.

"That's not like my Molly," I apologized to him.

It was a long drive home from the studio in downtown Memphis. Molly insisted that I take her to Cathy's.

That disappointment instilled in Molly a determination so fierce that nothing ever again would stand in her way. No matter what, whatever the price, she *would* be seen on TV. For that matter, all over the world.

And the price she paid was to give up her mother.

CHAPTER TWENTY-NINE

Brother-in-law Sued Me for Molly's Inheritance

Scheme One

M Y BEDEVILED BROTHER-IN-LAW BIL tried to persuade me to give him JJ's $100,000 life-insurance money, saying he needed to manage it for Molly—even though the will clearly stated that I was to keep JJ's personal life-insurance funds, which already had been dispersed to me.

Then I learned that JJ's Tennessee employer also had provided $50,000 for Molly, which the insurance manager Paul advised me. He added that BIL also had inquired about this payout, and Paul had told him the funds were being released to me, as Molly's custodial mother.

Then BIL had asked, "Well, what if Bonnie is no longer her custodial parent, then what?"

Paul had informed him that the funds would be disbursed to whomever the court appointed as legal guardian.

So BIL schemed.

Using JJ's attorney, Wampler, BIL asked the Court for a continuance of JJ's previous recent suit against me for sole custody of Molly. He asked that since her father had died, could Molly be adopted instead by a dear family friend of whom Molly was very fond?

Then BIL got Cathy to apply for full custody of Molly. Clearly, not for herself. There were a million other reasons.

Then Cathy while at work ran a credit report using Molly's social security number enticing she and BIL to apply for Molly's social security benefits. That's how he found out she was entitled to another $1,600 monthly while she was still a minor dependent child. Another incentive to get full custody.

BIL would get JJ's money, one way or another.

Scheme Two

BIL didn't want Molly living in JJ's house, where he himself had moved in when JJ went to the hospital the year before, in 2005.

With Molly out of the house, BIL was unencumbered in selling off all of JJ's art collection—which had been intended for Molly's college education—and all of JJ's belongings, as well as my own.

I had to use the proceeds from selling The Flannel Antler to pay for the court case, a custody fight for my own daughter.

However, *I* gave birth to Molly. You can change her name and her date of birth, but she is still *my* daughter.

The judge agreed. "My wife and fifteen-year-old daughter don't get along, either. They have disagreements all the time."

He turned to Molly. "Molly, this is your mother and your life has now been changed forever. You may not like it now but I feel it is in your best interest to return to your mother's care. I hereby remand that custody remain with the mother for her said minor child."

Literally, the judge had changed *nothing* from the divorce decree in 1999 that had awarded me as the sole-custodial parent of Molly.

Clang! The gavel went down, May 2006.

"Your honor," my attorney Bradley Ball asked, "may I ask, because of financial reasons that my client be allowed to re-turn to Colorado immediately to prepare the home for her daughter's arrival next month? It is a tremendous burden for her financially to remain here."

"Permission granted. The minor child will remain in Tennessee for the rest of the school year, to be returned upon completion of the ninth grade. So be it."

BIL shook his fist at me as he left the courtroom, cursing under his breath.

Amidst joyous tears, I thanked the judge, my lawyer, and God. I was allowed to keep custody of my daughter!

Molly tearfully embraced me. "I'm so sorry, Mommy, for all this trouble I have caused."

I hugged her with all my might. "It's okay, Molly. It's going to be alright."

CHAPTER THIRTY

Molly Disappeared

Back in Colorado, waiting for Molly to finish ninth grade and come home, my consumption of alcohol increased. More and more as each day passed.

I had lost my husband and the future we now would not enjoy. I had lost everything—but Molly.

Having sold The Flanner Antler, I now worked as the cafeteria lady at Granby's Middle Park High School, where Molly would attend when she came home.

Finally the month was up! At long last!

But, then, Molly didn't get off the plane.

I waited for what seemed like an eternity. When she didn't come dancing down the ramp toward me in typical Molly fashion and come running into my arms, confusion overwhelmed me. Then disbelief when the pilot, air hostess, and security all said she had never boarded.

Then Cathy's phone number was disconnected.

Then Sissy said they had moved without a forwarding address.

What had I done wrong this time?

As soon as I got home from the airport, the long long drive, I called the Grand County Police Department.

After a while, an officer rolled up in his patrol car. I ran out to meet him.

Standing beside his car, on the gravel drive, he said, "Your daughter didn't get off the plane?"

"No. In fact, she never got *on* the plane."

He leaned forward a bit and clearly smelled the alcohol on my breath.

I took in a breath and said, "She's disappeared. I tried her cell phone and her caretaker's phone, but no one is answering. Apparently, they moved and she is with them."

"Let me get this straight, you left her in Tennessee and now she won't come home? Is that right?"

"Well, sort of . . ."

He rubbed his chin and stared at me in my state of disarray. "How long has she been in Tennessee?"

"Ten months maybe."

He folded up his report book. "Well, ma'am, there's nothing we can do. She's a resident of Tennessee. You need to contact the Tennessee authorities."

I grabbed his wrist. He looked at me with a scowl, shook his wrist free, and entered his patrol car.

I grabbed hold of his rolled-down window. "Please, you've got to help me!" I held on tight to the window and walked alongside his moving vehicle.

He rolled up the window. "Let go of the window, Bonnie. And I suggest you sober up." And off he went.

So then I called the Memphis Police.

"Is this an emergency?"

"Well, not a 911 emergency. I want to file a missing person's report."

"You need to come into the station for that. We don't take reports over the phone."

"I'm in Colorado," I said, exasperation coming on. "I can't come into the station. My daughter is *missing*."

"Let me connect you. One moment."

"Memphis police."

"Hello, my name is Bonnie Brown. I used to live there, in Cordova. My daughter Molly Brown didn't get off the plane. . . " My words began to slur. ". . . And I can't find her."

"Where was she headed?"

"Home, to here in Colorado. This is her home." My tongue began to feel like it was growing thicker with each word I struggled to get out.

"How can I help you?"

"I want you to find my daughter. She's missing."

"Date of birth?"

"April 9, 1991. She just turned fifteen."

"How long has she been missing?"

"Since yesterday."

"Last known residence?"

"Well, she was staying with a friend. I spoke with them both yesterday. But now their phone is disconnected." I was beginning to nod off, as the alcohol effects were spreading through my brain. It was almost impossible to speak.

"Hmm. So your teenage daughter was visiting friends here in Memphis, but is a resident of Colorado and didn't come home? Is that right?"

"Well, yeah, sorta . . ." Why did I have to keep repeating this stuff over and over? Why wasn't anyone concerned?

"Hello?" the officer asked.

". . . Yes . . . I . . . am . . . here," I said slowly.

"I suggest you get hold of the friend she was staying with."

"That's why I'm calling you!" I yelled.

"You need to contact your local police. You are *not* in our jurisdiction. Besides, this is a civil matter that you need to handle with an attorney."

"I have an attorney, there in Memphis. I just spent a ton of money trying to get my daughter home."

"Again, there's nothing we can do."

CHAPTER THIRTY-ONE

Odd Jobs to Survive

F OR A MONTH, I lay in bed watching *Snapped* and stories about dead people, weeping for my sweet girl, my Molly Moo Moo girl.

Broken, I stayed drunk for days on end, for several weeks. I felt betrayed. My son went on a vision quest, my husband was dead, and my daughter had vanished. Boo-boo sopped up my relentless tears. She alone kept me alive because I had to care for her.

"Molly, oh Molly. Oh, bring my Molly back to me."

I slept in Molly's bed, next to the kitchen, drinking wine until I passed out night after night.

Occasionally, a friend checked up on me, to make sure I hadn't died. My new best friend owned the liquor store next to my house. Living between a bar and a liquor store was an alcoholic's dream.

I also was broke.

As I was no longer sought after as a highly skilled business woman, I took several odd jobs to make ends meet, and jobs in Grand Lake were scarce, especially for a woman.

I begged my way into a job at the Conoco gas station, part convenience store, part liquor store, where I got a discount. The owner had me running up and down the outside stairs, carrying up frozen products from the freezer below, and stocking the upstairs' cases. She had me constantly filling the coffee station, wiping it down, stocking, cleaning, dusting, and pumping gas, as well as sweeping inside and out. It was a nightmare, and way too much for a woman in her fifties, especially one with a drinking problem, although I didn't yet know I had one. My hourly wage was less than the $10 an hour I had paid my own staff when I was a store owner.

The worst part was that past customers would pop in and recognize me. They were polite but I was now a far cry from the vibrant, social, boutique owner they had once enjoyed. Rumors abound. I was no longer the darling of the community.

As all the women in Grand Lake, I worked two jobs. After the day job, I hustled over to Mavericks, a restaurant in Granby. I wasn't credited for being the retired chef for former President Ford. I had to work my way up, from washing dishes to waitress. And I had to carry heavy trays of food to the customers.

The last night on the job, I dropped the whole tray of food onto the floor because my arms were too weak to hold up the trays any longer.

Life was unbearable. I was barely alive.

And I couldn't get any help to find Molly.

Then a doctor diagnosed me with lung cancer.

I was depending on three bottles of wine to get me through every day.

CHAPTER THIRTY-TWO

My Elderly Mother—and Divine Intervention—Saved Me

G OD WAS MY PILOT. At age fifty-two, I survived by sleeping on my eighty-two year-old mother's sofa, a blow-up mattress, for an entire year before I could afford my own apartment. It was a desperate time. Very humbling after being married to a millionaire with a home of my own.

I arrived in northern Idaho in time for Thanksgiving 2008. It was my mom's loving care that helped me recover from alcohol abuse, and God.

Once I could get my own apartment, I was still back and forth dipping into the wine. June 2008 through November 2009, I had many jobs. One as house mom at the University of Idaho. Another as chef for the very prestigious Mrs. Mag-nuson; we didn't see eye to eye. Then at a casino in the deli/bingo hall. I was floundering.

Finally in 2009, I had a candid conversation with God: that if I gave up drinking alcohol, he would give me my daughter back.

The Promise

"No, I'm sure I do *not* need to go to a hospital," I declared that October to my brother Phil, who was living with Mom.

"Bonnie, your blood pressure is dangerously low," he said as the paramedics removed their equipment from my apartment. "You're going to die, and Mom will never forgive me."

"Leave me alone! Just let me be!" I pulled away from his grasp, as he was trying to get me to leave.

"Bonnie, we *all* love you and we're looking out for your best interest."

"No, you're not. You're just here because my neighbor called Mom. A friend of hers wants it, you know. She'll do anything to get me out of this apartment." I pushed Phil away from me and slid back onto the sofa, where I had been sitting before all this nonsense started.

"Thanks for coming," he apologized to the paramedics.

"No problem. That's our job." They all filed down the corridor of the apartment hallway.

Phil turned back to me. "Look, you must stop this. What happened? You've been sober for a year, and now this? Mom is worried sick about you. And it's not fair that I have to drive all the way over here, and you're not willing to accept the help you need."

"And let them stick needles and drip bags of saline into me? That's a $10,000 visit to the ER that I don't need. I can drink the Gatorade on my own very nicely, thank you."

"I'm done!" And out the door he went.

Soon after he left, the phone rang. "Bonnie, it's Mom. You need to stop this nonsense. You need to put the bottle down and go to bed, and get a good night's rest. I'll come tomorrow and we'll go shopping. We'll get some food in you. . . Bonnie, are you there?" she asked in a panic.

I wiped the tears from my eyes. "Okay, Mom. We'll do that."

I just wanted her to hold me and rock away my pain. She had never done that. Not because she hated me. She'd never had that kind of love herself.

Weary, I kneeled beside my bed, interlaced my fingers and prayed from the deepest core of my being, my voice frail.

"Please, Father, help me. I can't do this anymore. Please forgive me, for I know not what I do. Please don't let me continue harming myself.

"I know I'm dying. . . I just want to be with you and with my husband.

"Where's Molly? Why can't I find her? Is she there with you, Lord? Is she up there with her daddy?

"Please. I beg of you. I promise, if Molly is still here on this earth, if you'll help me find her, I promise I will never drink again, with your help. Please help me! I'm lost," I pleaded.

Instantly, warmth surged through my body. Then I retched for several hours.

The paramedics had said I was dehydrated and needed to drink Gatorade to restore my electrolytes, and had left a supply with me. So I forced down as much as I could, hugging a bowl and crying, my face red and hot, my hair soaked with perspiration from forcing myself to throw up.

After many hours, my hair damp and stringy, for the first time in a long time I wanted to take a shower—to cleanse away all the bad that had befallen me.

I pushed the bowl away and rose. I was shaky but more assured.

While lathering my hair for the much-needed shampoo, I found myself humming, "Amazing Grace that saved a wretch like me."

As I dried off, hopeful thoughts filled me and I realized I was standing without the assistance of the towel rack.

I surrendered to the angels and the call of the Lord.

Mom pulled up out front of my apartment. "Bonnie, you ready?" she hollered.

"On my way!" I said.

In the seat of Mom's new Honda, I felt my heavenly father's arms around me, in kindness, in love.

I no longer had that dead feeling in my soul. I was cooking my own recipes again, wonderful meals that nurtured me, now knowing that God had healed me.

CHAPTER THIRTY-THREE

IRS Found Molly!

IN 2015, I met with an AARP tax accountant. "Bonnie, your story about your missing daughter just broke my heart. This year, how about refiling your 2009 taxes, but this time," she continued, "we'll claim your child as a dependent. You're entitled, you know."

"Really? You can do that?" I said with a glimmer of hope.

"We can submit an amended return and maybe you can find out if your daughter is still alive."

"An amended return? I'm still in shock that I qualify as a senior citizen," I said, and we both chuckled.

JJ had always made more money than me. I was in a state for so many years that I wasn't the most stellar in filing my taxes. I had been reinventing myself *through* the alcoholism.

"In last year's returns, you didn't claim Molly on your taxes, right?" She entered all the information I provided. "Do you happen to have Molly's social security card with you?"

"Yes." I'd been carrying it since she disappeared.

"Okay, here we are. Molly Mackenzie Brown, born April 9, 1991, 532-XX-XXXX. There we go. All done. I hope you find your daughter, Bonnie. I hope this helps and that you will be able to reunite. Just sign here."

As I left the Coeur d' Alene Mall, April 7, 2015, my heart leapt! At last a break! And just two days before Molly's twenty-fourth birthday.

She was an adult now. If I could just find out if she was indeed alive. And if so, where she was.

I missed her so much! It had been such a long time!

A month later, I received my reimbursement for my qualifying child, Molly MacKenzie Brown.

Soon after that, my cell phone rang.

"Bonnie Brown?"

"Yes."

"This is agent XYZ with the Internal Revenue Service. Recently you filed an amended return with our offices."

"Yes, for 2009. I'm trying to find my daughter Molly. She went missing."

"Do you happen to have her Social Security card?" he asked.

"Yes."

"You need to bring both your card and hers to the Spokane Internal Revenue Office within the next two weeks."

After hanging up, I called my mom. "Mom, I'm in trouble! I filed an amended return for 2009, and now the IRS has called and I have to go in." I started sobbing.

"We'll get your affairs in order. Let's drive my car."

The IRS agent, Mom, and I were the only ones in the big echoing room. He was typing away at his computer behind the counter. I bit the inside of my cheek to keep from crying.

Then he glanced up at me and waved me over to his desk.

"I'm so sorry!" I blurted out as I sat in front of him. "I didn't mean to cause any harm. I give myself over to the authorities of the court. I surrender."

Mom started crying, too.

I leaned against the desk. "I just wanted to know if my daughter is alive. I just miss my daughter. I haven't been able to find her. I've searched and searched for eight years." I sobbed into a hankie and slid back in the chair. "Please go soft on me," I pleaded.

"Look, I don't know what you're talking about. You're Bonnie Brown, right?"

"Yes. . . ?"

"Do you have the social security cards?" He cocked an eyebrow, behind his thick-rimmed glasses.

I pulled out the cards and pushed them toward him on the desk.

He took them and typed faster. I turned and shrugged at Mom, who sat behind me.

"So, you're not going to arrest me?" I spewed.

"Arrest you? For what? Ha, ha, that's funny. Are you for real?" He said that without smiling and without taking his eyes off the computer screen.

I looked behind me at Mom and we both shrugged.

Still typing, he said, "You know you can change your name and your birthdate legally, don't you?"

"Sorry, what?"

"Your daughter has changed her name."

"Oh! She is alive!"

"Appears so."

I stared at his computer screen.

"See, Molly Mackenzie Brown." He held up her social security card. The numbers matched, *exactly*.

I sat back. "What does that mean? She changed her name? I just want her address."

He adjusted his glasses. "Umm, I can't give you her address. It's against HIPPA rules, because she's no longer a minor." He leaned in. "I *can* tell you her new name . . ."

"Okay, what is it?"

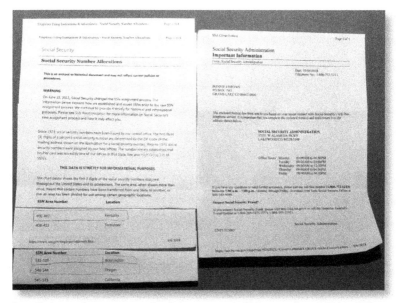

Jennifer's social security number beginning with 532 is not from KY but WA; where JJ, Bonnie, Cody, and Molly resided.

"Jennifer Shrader Lawrence."

My heart stopped. What? . . . She had hated her school-friend Jennifer. And she chose Kayla Shrader's last name as her new middle name hence deleting the "c". She had changed her birthday? I looked at Mom. Then back at the agent. "Are you absolutely positive she's my daughter? And would you please tell your boss I need her address?"

I stood, frustrated and anxious. Jennifer Shrader Lawrence, huh?

"I must know the truth," I insisted to him. "She's been missing. My daughter is *missing.*"

"Not anymore."

"Please, I beg you. Can you give me anything more? *Where* she is?"

"I suggest you hire a private investigator. Or look her up on the Internet."

"I don't have a computer," I said, embarrassed.

"They have them at the library."

CHAPTER THIRTY-FOUR

Family and Friends Knew Before I Did

IMMEDIATELY AFTER LEAVINg, Mom and I went to a library, and I accessed the Internet and discovered that the beautiful woman Jennifer Shrader Lawrence was *my* Molly MacKenzie Brown! I danced, jubilant.

Back at home in Hayden, I called my sis. "Lorraine! I have incredible news! You're not going to believe this! Can I come over?"

"Sure. Harvey's resting."

It was a warm May morning. We sat on her porch swing, overlooking her beautiful mature gardens. She made us lemonade. I could hardly sit still, squirming in the seat, grinning ear to ear.

"Well, what's going on?"

I leaned in and gripped Lorraine's arm. "I found Molly! She is very much alive! *And* she is an *actress!* A good one, too!"

"What?"

"Yep. Mom and I went to the IRS office and the agent told me that Jennifer Shrader Lawrence has the *same* social security number as Molly! She changed her name *and* birthdate."

"That's ridiculous," Lorraine proclaimed and stood up off the swing. Then she confessed that Molly had called her. "Molly is in college studying to be an art teacher. I even offered to let her come and stay with us, but she politely refused. The last time she called, she asked me to send baby pictures and school photos. And I did. She said you have all her photos and she needed them. So, I sent her a couple of duplicates."

"Lorraine! You *knew* Molly was alive and you didn't tell me? How could you do this? Sisters are supposed to love one another, not withhold information."

"Molly has called me several times over the last seven years," Lorraine said apologetically. "She wanted to make sure you were alive. She wanted to know about your sobriety and recovery. Bonnie, I swear. I thought she was just Molly, protecting her anonymity."

"She's the actress in THE HUNGER GAMES, Lorraine."

A light came on in Lorraine's eyes. "The last time she called was in 2010 after *Winter's Bone*, just before *The Hunger Games* came out.

Lorraine saw my disappointment in her. ". . . I only just found out. . . I promise."

She looked so regretful that I couldn't hold it against her. I sighed. "What address did you send them to? Do you have a phone number?"

"No. It's on an old computer we got rid of."

At that moment, I felt hope slipping away from me.

I injured my shoulder in 2013 and had to leave my job as a cashier at Sears, to have rotator cuff surgery. That's when I learned I could go to school and get a degree using student loans. So, I was all in.

I bought my first laptop at age fifty-nine to type my studies and term papers. It took my mind off missing Molly.

Most of my fellow students were Molly's age. I enjoyed their youth and had a relationship with many of them.

English classes gave me the ability to write this book.

I returned to Grand Lake, Colorado in June 2015. I needed to get to the bottom of Molly being Jennifer Shrader

Lawrence, and to visit Molly's friends Kayla and Heather Schrader. Mom lent me money so I could rent a U-Haul and bring my furniture and belongings back to Idaho.

It was my first time back since 2008, and now I was sober.

Heather Schrader was working as Assistant Manager at the Grand Lake Lodge. I hadn't seen her in seven years. Since she used to call me Mom and I felt like she was Molly's sister, as she'd been at our house every day, I went to the Lodge one day for lunch.

She came up to the table and hugged me. "Mom is that you? What are you doing here?"

"Well, I came to see you, Heather. I've missed Grand Lake, and you and your sister. It's been a long and lonely seven years. I'm sober now."

"Oh, that's so good. No one knew what happened to you, just that you lost everything after your auction, then disappeared."

"I went to live with Molly's grandma. She got me sober. I'm a better person now."

Then Heather, too, admitted that she'd had contact with Molly in 2011.

I was disappointed that Molly hadn't reached out to me, also. Yet happy that she was still in touch with her dearest friend.

"It must make you feel special, Heather," I said with genuine joy for her, "that she's adopted your last name?"

"Yes, but she deleted the 'c' so you couldn't find her."

I wondered why, with a moment of sorrow. But at least now I knew for sure that Molly was, indeed, the actress Jennifer Lawrence.

Molly girl!

My heart filled with relief that at last I had found her. Also sadness at the many lost years. Also happiness that she had found the life she'd always wanted.

Molly girl, I am so proud of you!

CHAPTER THIRTY-FIVE

The Even More Diabolical Plan: Scheme Three

HAVING CUSTODY OF MOLLY, BIL no longer needed Cathy. He fired her and rekindled his friendship with a woman JJ had apparently dated, Karen Lawrence, the horse trainer, according to the photo JJ left behind.

Through my research he hired Karen as Molly's new caretaker and paid her to convince my *minor* child into leaving her life, making Molly promise never to contact me again.

So, Molly moved with Karen to Louisville, Kentucky to continue equestrian camp, not in Tennessee where she had trained all the years before.

From articles about Jennifer that I've pieced together, she (Molly) had to clean the horse stalls after she got to Kentucky and Karen told her she could no longer ride the horses. "You have to clean up after the rich people now."

And Molly had answered, "That's not what I signed up for."

By that time, she had to babysit in order to earn money. It was not a summer vacation.

I'd had five-years of sobriety when I discovered that Karen, at BIL's bidding, was hiding Molly from me.

I wrote Karen, her mother and her sister, begging them to let me have a relationship with Molly.

No response.

In June 2016, trying to reach out to my daughter, I visited Jennifer Lawrence's house in L.A. The guard at the entrance called the P.A., who said, "We don't know a Bonnie Brown. Send her away."

Not taking no for an answer, I drove to Jennifer's old apartment in Santa Monica, from when she had acted in *The Bill Engvall Show* in 2008.

Out of the ten mailboxes the Lawrence's were number nine. At the small gate, I pushed the button. No one answered. As I stood outside the gate a tenant walked-up, and miraculously let me enter.

I knocked on the door. No answer. I stood there, wondering what to do.

A woman next door came out. "They're not home right now."

"Well, I'm just looking for Jennifer."

"She hasn't lived here for a very long time. She lives up in the hills now. The only people who come here are Karen and her friends, but they haven't been here in about six months." She paused. "Can you hold on a second?"

She came back to the door and handed me a letter. "Will you give it to Jennifer next time you see her? It ended up in my mailbox. I've been very ill, just had surgery, but I want to make sure she gets it.

"Sure and thank you"

It was a year later after I wrote the book that I opened that envelope inadvertently. It was an income-tax statement for a company named Floffin—with Karen Lawrence as Treasurer. That's when I discovered that Karen might be double-dipping. It looked as though she was receiving a monthly salary as Molly's agent? (2006 to the present?), from the Floffin deposits from Jennifer's *residuals*. Each month, Molly/Jennifer was paying *two* paychecks to Karen, from both her inheritance and from the newly formed business, which Karen had started when Molly was sixteen. (*Research gained from the world-wide web—see page 174*).

Was this how Karen could take her entire family to Europe in 2008 for Jennifer's movie premier in Italy of *The Poker House*, a movie I *never* would have approved, about a wayward teenage girl raped by her sister's pimp.

And while they were in Rome, where were the adults? There are pictures of Karen's own college-age son, Blaine, carrying an underage, drunk Jennifer over his shoulder. She was seventeen. Just because Karen had made Molly a year older to hide her identity didn't make it so. Jennifer is a year *younger* than stated on her SAG card. And how did SAG let that one slip by? Also, she was not born in August. That's when her father died.

It's also reported that Jennifer knocked on doors to modeling agencies in New York. They were interested, but she walked out, determined to be an actress. She was watching street performers when a photographer came up and said, "There's a part available in L.A. Can I have your phone number? I'll call you tomorrow if they like your photographs."

She gave him Karen's number.

The next morning, he called Karen. "I met your daughter yesterday. Took photographs of her. Gave them to a producer. And he wants to do screen test with her. So, I'm providing a plane ticket to L.A. for her, you, your husband and Blaine for her screen test. What do you think of that?"

Still not giving up, I drove five miles further to Jennifer's public-relations firm, ID, in L.A. They were getting her real, solid movie parts, like *Winter's Bone*, then the *Hunger Games*.

I sat in the lobby for several hours on a white-leather couch, waiting to be called to the office, so I could prove once and for all, with evidence in hand—birth certificate, social security number, and childhood photographs—that Jennifer Lawrence is my daughter, Molly, who was absconded from me at age fifteen.

Finally after five p.m., the security guard made one final call to the office and handed me the phone.

"No," the receptionist growled at me, "I told you. You need an appointment."

"But, ma'am, I have all the evidence to prove Jennifer Lawrence is my daughter."

"And I told you, YOU NEED AN APPOINTMENT." She slammed down the phone.

"But . . . but that's why I'm here. . . to get an appointment."

Tears flooded down my cheeks as the security guard showed me out the door.

I walked down their red carpet past the shiny elevators along the paparazzi wall to the underground parking.

Next, Wilshire Boulevard at the Time Warner, Inc. office. They had security guards. too.

A janitor in the back took pity on me and called a friend at *People* magazine.

"No, she's just left on vacation," the receptionist told me.

"Well, I received a response to my query, stating that someone would get hold of me. I'm here now. Down in the lobby."

"What's your name?"

"Bonnie Brown."

"You've got five seconds, Bonnie Brown," she said hurriedly, "to tell me why you're bothering me on a Friday night at five p.m."

"I am Jennifer Lawrence's birth mother. I sent your office a photograph of her as a young girl. I was hoping that by traveling to L.A. in person, you would realize I have a serious concern for her welfare—*and* a great story."

She stopped me. "Well, consider your three minutes up. We'll call you if the editor is interested. She just left on a two-week vacation overseas." Click.

After my visit to L.A., Karen hired Hodgson a reporter who sold an article to HEAT magazine 2016 stating I went to KY. and banged on their door demanding Jennifer come outside. I've never been to Kentucky. If I was Karen I would have called the cops? She can't, it would prove I am her mom via a DNA test.

Why not let Jennifer make the decision? I wondered. It was in her best interest, not those who were getting rich off of her.

So, I returned to my Coeur d Alene apartment not ready to give up. Just to find a new strategy.

Two weeks later, I met a girl Jennifer's age, whose family owned *Jennifer's* favorite horse OREO from Kentucky and they had just put up the horse for sale. What were the odds? This young adolescent had gone to Camp Hi Ho with my Molly during the summers She knew her as Jennifer, as Karen's daughter—as Jennifer Shrader Lawrence.

That's why none of Jennifer's real classmates have ever been found. Because there are none. She did *not* attend Kam-merer Middle School. Here's how that story started:

Karen Lawrence had persuaded a teacher to arrange a photo opportunity for Jennifer at the school, so she would have a school history because Jennifer had none. Karen plied the teacher with a very large donation to the school as told to me by a current employee at the school.

Then Karen added Kammerer Middle School to a bogus lineage for Jennifer, which included a fake grandfather, a pre-tend aunt and cousins.

None of it was real. And it was all posted online at *MyFamilyTree.com.*

In talking with the higher ups at Kammerer Middle School, they regretted the day Jennifer came to their school, and said the teacher had been fired.

In 2015, I challenged *Celebrity Yearbooks*, making them prove to me that the high school photo they had sold to *People* magazine was, in fact, Jennifer Lawrence. I asked if they had extracted it from an *actual* yearbook, or if the grainy photo had been submitted to them by Karen Lawrence.

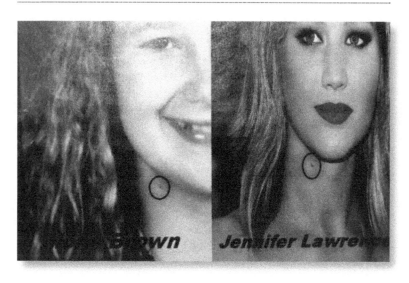

They threatened me—but the photo soon disappeared. Jennifer admitted in her 60 minutes interview on national TV January 2018 she never attended high school. One good thing the photo did accom-plish: it shows the mole on Molly's neck, *identical* to Jennifer Lawrence's mole.

Back home in Colorado, I found my box of over two-hundred photographs of Molly, which I had taken home from JJ's estate sale. I had left them at the cabin when I moved to Idaho in 2008, because they were painful reminders.

Plenty of the photos show that *Jennifer Lawrence* really went to East Grand Middle School in Granby, Colorado—as Molly Mackenzie Brown.

Amidst these photographs, I came across a *single* picture of what experts believe is Molly's equestrian teacher—Karen Lawrence—being embraced by JJ and it wasn't just a hug.

That's when I began sending letters. First to Karen. To Jennifer's fake grandfather. To the pretend Aunt Cindy and cousins. To Camp Hi Ho.

I had my work cut out for me. They had everything to lose if Jennifer's true identity was revealed.

CHAPTER THIRTY-SIX

Journal

I KEPT A DAILY JOURNAL the entire time Molly was missing to me, 2006-2015. Writing about how much I missed her kept me going. It kept her alive.

I filled several notebooks.

In January 2016, I took a workshop with Jack Castle on "How to Publish Your Book." When I shared my synopsis and prologue with him, he asked me if the story was true.

"Well, yes. That's what nonfiction means."

"Then you *have* to write this book!" he exclaimed. "The world deserves to know the real story of Jennifer Lawrence's young life and how she really got to be who she is today."

I never gave up trying to find my daughter. It was an achingly long time.

Until 2017 . . .

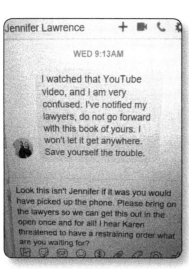

Jennifer Lawrence + 🎥 📞 ⚙

WED 9:13AM

I watched that YouTube video, and I am very confused. I've notified my lawyers, do not go forward with this book of yours. I won't let it get anywhere. Save yourself the trouble.

Look this isn't Jennifer if it was you would have picked up the phone. Please bring on the lawyers so we can get this out in the open once and for all! I hear Karen threatened to have a restraining order what are you waiting for?

Jennifer Lawrence + 🎥 📞 ⚙

10:48AM

You can't sell this book. You need to stop this.
-J

4BYE4 How
Molly Brown.
This is the sto...
youtube.com

12:22PM

Its the only way I know to get you to reunite. I dont

Jennifer Lawrence + 🎥 📞 ⚙ ✕

I would like to apologize for the rude way you were spoken to last month. The person who has used my account has since been spoken with and consequences have been applied. It it not. nor has it ever been my intention to have this account used for anything other than a loving connections with fans, friends, and family. Take care. ♥

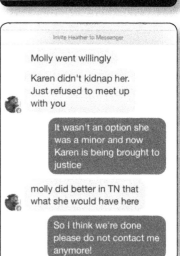

Invite Heather to Messenger

Molly went willingly

Karen didn't kidnap her. Just refused to meet up with you

It wasn't an option she was a minor and now Karen is being brought to justice

molly did better in TN that what she would have here

So I think we're done please do not contact me anymore!

CHAPTER THIRTY-SEVEN

Fan Page Private Messages

"Tell the truth, or someone will tell it for you."
–STEPHANIE KLEIN, *Straight Up and Dirty*

AFTER THE ILLUMINATING VISIT with Heather Schrader in 2015, I started my own Facebook timeline. I also started going to see all of Jennifer's movies, and I took all of the cinema and theatrical classes I could at North Idaho College. Once reunited with Molly (Jennifer), I wanted to be able to speak her new language. Movies. So she would know how proud I am of her.

That November, I began sending PM to Jennifer's FB private messages.

In 2016, I started a Facebook Page, where I posted pictures of Molly/Jennifer as a little girl. Some readers made up stories, saying they knew my daughter Jennifer, or that they were classmates with Jennifer's faux-mother, the only one the world knew—up until now.

Karen Lawrence found my FB Page and saw how I was letting the world know that JL is *my* Molly. Karen started Photoshopping *my* pictures off *my* Facebook Page and leaking them to the media, writing, "This is the high-school picture of JL. . . This is a picture of Jennifer when she was a little girl. . ."

2017 is when Facebook brought us together.

I began receiving Facebook Fan Page *private messages.* I knew they were from Jennifer, because she would do a line and a capital J—which was Molly's signature for her daddy JJ.

May 2017, in a private message, Jennifer sent me: *Happy Mother's Day.*

December 2017: *Scolding someone for being mean to Bonnie.*

Early January 2018, I added Jennifer to my Facebook messenger, where I began giving her light motherly advice: things I had noticed, concern that she was drinking so much, getting a reputation I worried was hurting her.

She wrote back: *You have just given me the best idea in a long time.*

Me: *I'm glad I could be of service. Let me know how I was able to help you.*

Jen: *Oh, yeah, this really gave me a great idea.*

The next week, Jennifer announced publically that she was going to take a year off from acting.

Was that what I had encouraged her to do? I had been encouraging her to spend some time sorting out the drinking, plus she hadn't had time to grieve her father.

The next week she announced she was in therapy. Was she listening to what I was telling her? I thought therapy was a brilliant idea. I'd been working with my own psychotherapist. In fact, she had helped me realize JJ was a sociopath.

Then, Jennifer announced—on *60 Minutes*—that she had lied. She had not gone to high school after ninth grade.

January 30, 2018 was the day everything changed and I knew for sure I had found Molly.

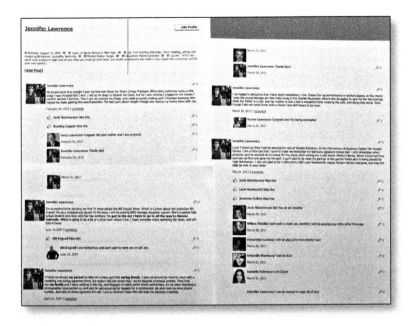

I was at my bank when a message popped up in Facebook on my brand-new cell phone:

From JL, thanking me for the message I had sent her.

We then very loosely chatted back and forth for a bit. I said something like, "Oh, that's really funny," and we exchanged a couple of messages.

I love you, Molly Girl, I wrote.

She immediately replied, *I love you, too, Mom.*

My heart brimming with the thrill of the moment, I showed it to the bank manager.

Then, crying, I wrote back to Jennifer:

That's the best thing you've said to me in a very long time.

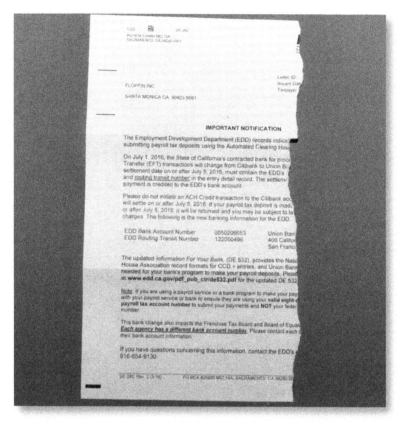

The income tax statement for Floffin, Inc.: *"I only had a pen and no paper so finding my daughter not there I ripped off the corner of the letter the neighbor just gave me—Molly girl Jen I wrote 'whenever you find this know I love you and only want the best for you! Call me.' I placed it in the palm tree at the 5'9" height I knew my girl would see sticking out from the palm frond."* –BONNIE BROWN—notice the password for the account, 532, matches Jennifer's/Molly's Social Security Number prefix.

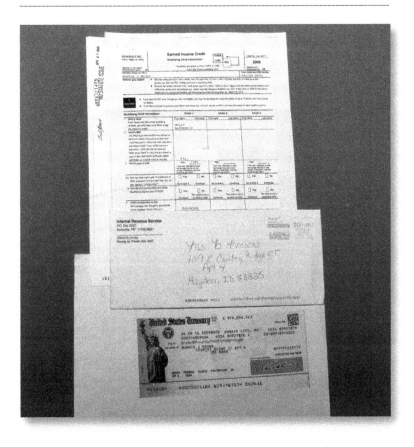

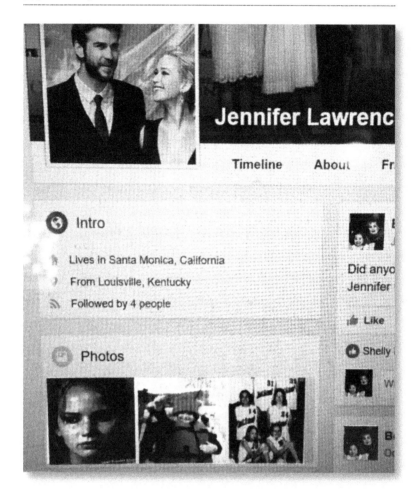

"*How hurtful it can be to deny one's true self and live a life of lies just to appease others.*"

–JUNE AHERN